THE
WELL-DECORATED
GARDEN

THE
WELL-DECORATED
GARDEN

MAKING OUTDOOR ORNAMENTS AND ACCENTS

LAURA DOVER DORAN

LARK BOOKS

ASHEVILLE, NORTH CAROLINA

BOOK AND COVER DESIGN, PHOTOSTYLING, AND PRODUCTION:
Chris Bryant

PHOTOGRAPHY:
Evan Bracken

EDITORIAL ASSISTANCE:
Heather Smith
Catharine Sutherland

PRODUCTION ASSISTANCE:
Hannes Charen
Val Anderson

ILLUSTRATIONS:
Orrin Lungren (line art)
Laura Roberson (on chapter openers and pages 7 and 128)

for
Ella

Library of Congress Cataloging-in-Publication Data

Doran, Laura Dover, 1970–

    The well-decorated garden : making outdoor ornaments and accents / Laura Dover Doran.—1st ed.
       p. cm.
    Includes index.
    ISBN 1-57990-106-9
    1. Woodwork. 2. Garden ornaments and furniture
    3. Garden structures I. Title.
    TT180.D63 1999
    684.1'8—dc21   98-48216
                                          CIP

10 9 8 7 6 5 4 3 2

Published by Lark Books
50 College Street
Asheville, NC 28801
USA

© 1999, Lark Books

For information about distribution in the U.S., Canada, the U.K., Europe, and Asia, call Lark Books at 828-253-0467.

Distributed in Australia by Capricorn Link (Australia) Pty Ltd., P.O. Box 6651, Baulkham Hills Business Centre, NSW 2153, Australia

Distributed in New Zealand by Southern Publishers Group, 22 Burleigh St., Grafton, Auckland, NZ

Printed in China by L. Rex Printing Company, Ltd.

ISBN 1-57990-106-9

Contents

the Well-Decorated GARDEN

Introduction

Gardens are as unique as the people who tend them, and most gardeners share a desire to create an outdoor space that is an extension of the home, a place to work and relax. Just as every gardener has different ideas of what plants to grow, notions of what should adorn the garden space vary widely. A Victorian birdhouse may be the perfect addition to a small cottage flower bed; by the same token, a pair of stately metal urns positioned at an entryway anticipates the formality of a stately knot garden. Whether you decorate your garden with furniture to create an outdoor living or dining space or simply place an attractive stepping stone among your flowers, you will have made your garden more familiar and inviting.

Whatever your style, if you have taken the time to create a garden, you probably already know the enjoyment of finding the perfect garden ornament. Browse through these pages and see how easy it is to experience the satisfaction of making one yourself. I've selected projects that utilize a wide variety of techniques and skill levels, everything from charming rustic plant markers, to impressive garden torches made of metal screening, to a colorful garden table that requires only basic woodworking skills.

You've planned,
you've plowed,
you've planted.
Now for the decorative touch...

Garden Containers

GARDEN GLOVE PLANTERS

F*abric stiffener transforms ordinary cotton garden gloves into colorful waterproof containers. They make functional planters, adorable posy holders, or simple decorative elements for both home and garden.*

DESIGNER: **Anne McCloskey**

Materials and Tools

Cotton garden gloves

Fabric stiffener

Acrylic varnish or primer

Acrylic paints in assorted colors:
  fuchsia, lavender, light pink,
  pink, light green, dark green,
  peach, and yellow

Exterior polyurethane

Plastic insects

Cotton twine, approximately
  1 yard (.9 m) per glove

Plastic bags and plastic wrap

Assorted paintbrushes

Foam brush

Strong-bonding adhesive

Electric drill

Floral wire

Instructions

1 To stiffen gloves, pour a generous amount of stiffener into a plastic bag and add one glove at a time to the bag, completely saturating each glove.

2 Stuff each glove with crumpled plastic bags and lay the gloves on plastic wrap. Take care to open the top of the glove enough to form a flower container, and position the thumb on each glove so that it curves inward toward the palm (see photograph). Remember: position gloves carefully at this point; this is your only chance to get the desired arrangement. Allow stiffener to dry completely.

3 Apply acrylic varnish or primer to both sides of the glove, one side at a time, and allow to dry thoroughly. Remove plastic bags.

4 Paint designs on gloves, either free-hand or as described below.

To paint the FUCHSIA GLOVE (top), first paint the cuff of the glove lavender. Paint the body of the glove fuchsia, one side at a time, allowing the first side to dry thoroughly before turning the glove over. Allow to dry thoroughly. Beginning at the top of the glove and working down, paint pink teardrop-shaped roses all over the surface of one side of the glove. Use a small brush to highlight the side of the rosebud with light pink paint, then paint a light green leaf under each bud. Outline the leaf with dark green paint. Allow to dry thoroughly, then repeat with the other side of the glove.

To paint the PINK GLOVE (bottom), first paint the cuff of the glove yellow. Paint the body of the glove pink, one side at a time, allowing the first side to dry thoroughly before turning the glove over. Allow to dry thoroughly. Beginning at the top of the glove and working down on one side, paint five light pink dots to form a flower outline, then fill in centers of flowers with a dot of yellow paint. Paint simple leaf shapes next to the flowers, filling in the design as you work. Allow to dry thoroughly, then repeat with the other side of the glove.

5 Apply at least two coats of exterior polyurethane to both sides of both gloves. With a foam brush, apply a coat of fabric stiffener to the inside of each glove. (This coats the inside, so that the gloves may be used as a planter.)

6 Glue a plastic insect to the collar of each glove with strong-bonding adhesive, and allow to dry.

7 Drill two holes in the top of each glove. Cut the cotton twine into two pieces, then wrap pieces of twine with floral wire. Insert ends of twine through the holes in the gloves, then knot ends twice. Note: Wrapping ends of twine with clear tape will make the twine easier to insert.

8 If you are using your gloves as planters, fill them with small stones for drainage, use a light soil mixture, and plant.

PICKET FENCE PLANTER

N othing conjures the charm of a country garden like a picket fence. This planter holds three 6-inch (15-cm) pots. See page 12 for instructions on making the painted seed packets.

Materials and Tools

½-inch-thick wood for pickets: 34 pieces, each 1½ x 9 inches

¾-inch-thick wood for planter frame: Four 5½- x 1-inch pieces, four 24- x 1-inch pieces, and one 22½- x 1-inch piece

Exterior wood primer/sealer, white

Exterior semigloss latex paint, green

Pencil

Saw

Wood glue

¾-inch (2-cm) brads

Hammer

Sandpaper

Paintbrush

Instructions

1 Cut the picket tops by marking ½ inch (1.5 cm) from each corner and 2 inches (5 cm) down the sides on one short end of each piece. Draw the lines with a pencil and cut the angles.

2 Position two 24-inch frame pieces with two 5½-inch pieces at each end. Glue, then brad these pieces together as shown in the diagram. Repeat this process with the remaining 24-inch and 5½-inch pieces. Glue and brad the 22½-inch piece inside the bottom frame assembly (see diagram), equally spaced from the sides, to create a supporting brace.

3 Set the two frame assemblies on their ends. Position one slat flush with each corner of the bottom frame and move the top frame flush to the edge 6¾ inches (17 cm) from the bottom. Glue and brad in position. Repeat at the other end.

4 Lay the assembly on its side. Position a picket slat at each end so that each picket is flush with the end slats. Glue and brad in position.

5 Place the remaining picket slats around the frame so that they are equally spaced and secure with glue and brads.

6 Sand all surfaces. Paint entire planter with white primer and allow to dry thoroughly.

7 Paint planter with green semigloss paint. When paint has thoroughly dried, rub over all exposed surfaces with coarse sandpaper to create a distressed look.

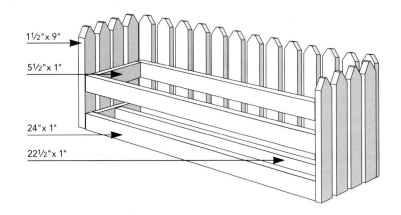

1½" x 9"

5½" x 1"

24" x 1"

22½" x 1"

DESIGNER: **Robin Clark**

ARTIST'S
GALLERY

Bob Keegan

Bob Keegan is an alpine folk artist who has sculpted over ten thousand faces in wood and rock. His alpine garden sculptures are created by hand from igneous rock quarried in the Sierra Mountains. He learned this technique by studying with folk artists in Austria.

ALPINE GARDEN SCULPTURE
Carved lava rock
PHOTO: Lois Keegan

PAINTED SEED PACKETS

DESIGNER: **Anne McCloskey**

These colorful, hand-painted seed packets add a whimsical touch to the garden when suspended from planters (see page 11) or wreaths, or attached to stakes and used as markers for seed plantings. As Christmas tree ornaments, they are a delightful reminder of the spring to come.

Materials and Tools

Six 3½- x 5-inch (9- x 12.5-cm) wood plaques with beveled edges (available at craft supply stores)

Acrylic glaze or wood primer

Acrylic paints in assorted colors: white and black as well as various shades of blue, yellow, green, pink, orange, and brown

Fine-point permanent black marker

¾-yard (.7-m) lengths of ribbon in assorted colors/styles, ¾ inch (2 cm) wide

Exterior polyurethane

Assorted paintbrushes

Pencil

Sponge

Thumbtacks

Tacky glue

Instructions

1 To paint the seed packets, you will need a square brush to paint the backgrounds, and a round-tip brush for detail work. Begin by coating the front and back of all wood plaques with clear acrylic glaze or other wood primer. Allow glaze or primer to dry thoroughly.

2 Paint the front and back of the plaques a color of your choice (use photograph as a guide). Allow paint to dry thoroughly.

3 Measure 1½ inches (4 cm) from the top of the plaque and make a light pencil line. Paint the top section (above the line) a color of your choice—again, refer to the photograph. Sponge the sides of the plaque lightly with paint.

4 Measure from the top of the painted top section about three-fourths of the way down and mark with a pencil. Carefully pencil in the name of the flower, then go over penciled letters with a permanent marker. Erase any visible pencil marks. Repeat this process for each seed packet.

5 Paint individual flowers on seed packets, either freehand or as directed on page 14.

6 Waterproof by glazing both sides of each seed packet with exterior polyurethane.

7 Fold ribbon lengths in half and thumbtack center of ribbon (at fold) to the back of the plaque to create a hanger. Place a dab of tacky glue around thumbtack to secure. Tie ends of ribbon into a bow. Repeat for all seed packets.

For the PETUNIA seed packet, the body of the plaque is yellow, and the top border is light blue. Paint green leaves in the upper and lower left portions of the plaque, blending dark green paint around the outer edges and centers of the leaves and adding white paint for highlights. First, paint a white flower. Use a pencil to mark 10 triangular sections on the flower. Paint alternating sections fuchsia. Dab yellow paint in the center of the flower, then make light pink streaks radiate from the center. Paint white lines around center and middle of flower center (accent with black), then paint pink lines on fuchsia sections and fuchsia lines on white sections of flower. Add a green stem and a white flower bud to the upper right section of the plaque.

For the COSMOS seed packet, the body of the plaque is light pink, and the top border is fuchsia. First, paint the green leaves in the lower left corner of the plaque, blending dark green paint around the edges of leaves. Add a small amount of white paint for highlights. Use lavender and purple for the flower petals, blending paints from the outside inward. Softly outline inner petals and edges of flower with white paint. Paint center dark yellow and dot with black. Highlight the center of the flower with white paint. Add green stems and purple flower buds in the upper right section of the plaque.

For the MARIGOLD seed packet, the body of the plaque is fuchsia, and the top border is lavender. Paint green leaves in the lower left and upper right portions of the plaque (see photograph), blending dark green paint around the outer edges and centers of the leaves and adding white paint for highlights. Use dark yellow and light yellow paint to make the flowers, blending both yellows into the centers of the flowers. Dot black paint in the center of each flower. Add green stems and flower buds in the upper right and left sections of the plaque.

For the SUNFLOWER seed packet, the body of the plaque is periwinkle, and the top border is dark yellow. Paint a dark brown circle in the center of the bottom portion of the plaque. Swirl olive green, brown, and light brown paint into circle to create the center of the flower. Make small black dots in the middle of the flower center. Use dark and light yellow paint to make the flower petals, stroking outward from the center with a square paintbrush.

For the ZINNIA seed packet, the body of the plaque is orange, and the top border is light pink. Begin by painting green leaves in the lower portion of the plaque, blending dark green paint around the outer edges and centers of the leaves. Add white paint for highlights. Use fuchsia and light pink paint to make flower petals; paint three rows of petals around center of flower. Dab yellow-green and light yellow paint in the center of the flower; dot in black. Add a green stem and flower bud (with fuchsia and light pink paint) in the upper right section of the plaque.

For the PANSY seed packet, the body of the plaque is light blue, and the top border is light green. Begin by painting green leaves in the lower left corner of the plaque, blending dark green paint around the outer edges and centers of the leaves. Add a small amount of white paint for highlights. Use lavender and white paint to make two pansies, flattening the paintbrush and pulling it into the center of each flower. Paint dark yellow circles inside each flower, then use a permanent marker to draw lines inside pansies. Add green stems and flower buds (with lavender, white, and periwinkle paint) in the upper right section of the plaque. Dot buds with yellow, green, and white paint.

FAUX GRANITE PLANTER

One of the wonderful aspects of decorative painting is that you can match the painted finish to your individual garden setting. Here, we've used the colors of natural stones—black and shades of taupe—to create a granite finish. Grays and tans can also be added. If you have a lot of terra cotta in your garden, try a red or salmon-colored granite design.

DESIGNER: **Gay Grimsley**

Materials and Tools

Wooden planter

Exterior wood primer

Exterior latex semigloss paint: black, light taupe, and dark taupe

Exterior spray polyurethane

Fine sandpaper

Paintbrush

Paint tray

Small sea sponge

Small artist's paintbrush

Instructions

1 Sand the wooden planter to remove any rough edges.

2 Prime planter with exterior primer to seal the wood and to prevent knots from bleeding through the finish. Prime the inside and bottom of the planter as well. Allow to dry thoroughly, then lightly sand entire planter again. (*Note:* If the planter is redwood, you will need to use an oil-based sanding sealer [thinned oil varnish]; otherwise, a water-based primer can be used.)

3 Apply two coats of black paint to the sides and bottom of the planter and two coats of light taupe on the inside. Allow planter to dry thoroughly between coats.

4 Pour a small amount of dark taupe paint into a paint tray, then add an equal amount of water to thin the paint. Dip a moistened sea sponge lightly into the paint and dab sponge into the paint tray to release excess paint. (The sponge should have very little paint on it.)

DISTRESSED PLANTER

5 Lightly dab the sponge over the entire planter, changing directions to achieve varied imprints from the sponge. Sponge paint on heavier in some areas so color is not too consistent.

6 Use a small artist's brush to lightly dab the paint into the corners and recesses of the planter that the sponge did not cover.

7 Mix a small amount of the light taupe paint into the dark taupe paint to achieve a medium taupe shade. Add an equal amount of water to thin the paint. Sponge and brush on this color, using the same method as described in steps 5 and 6 above.

8 Mix equal parts of light taupe paint and water and apply this color, using the same method as described in steps 5 and 6 above.

9 If necessary, go back and add any of the colors (or additional colors) until you achieve the desired effect. Allow paint to dry thoroughly.

10 Apply four to five coats of polyurethane, letting dry between coats. Make sure you spray the inside and bottom of the planter as well.

11 If necessary, insert a plastic liner inside the planter or drill holes in the bottom to allow water to drain.

Depending on the style of the garden, it is sometimes preferable to create garden containers that look aged. Here, we used paint to "weather" a plain wooden planter so that it is at home among rusty metal chairs with flaking paint.

DESIGNER: **Sharon Tompkins**

Materials and Tools

Wooden planter

Exterior wood primer

Exterior latex semigloss paint:
    red, green, and ivory

White craft glue

Oil or latex wood stain, walnut
    (optional)

Exterior spray polyurethane

Fine sandpaper

Paintbrush

Plastic bucket

Clean rags (optional)

Moist black dirt (optional)

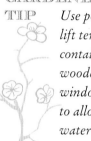

GARDENER'S
TIP   *Use pot feet to
lift terra-cotta
containers or
wooden
windowboxes
to allow for
water drainage
and ventilation.*

Instructions

1 Sand the wooden planter to remove any rough edges.

2 Prime planter with exterior primer to seal the wood and to prevent knots from bleeding through the finish. Prime the inside and bottom of the planter as well. Allow to dry thoroughly, then lightly sand entire planter again. (*Note*: If the planter is redwood, you will need to use an oil-based sanding sealer [thinned oil varnish]; otherwise, a water-based primer can be used.)

3 Coat planter with red latex paint and allow to dry thoroughly.

4 Pour white glue into a plastic bucket, thin slightly with water, then brush diluted glue onto planter. (The mixture should be approximately four parts glue to one part water.) As the glue sets up, it will begin to sag. Brush glue out until it begins to stiffen. Allow glue to dry for at least two to three hours, preferably overnight.

5 Apply the next color of paint (green) in even strokes in one direction. Don't worry about covering planter perfectly at this point, and don't spread the paint around, because it will lift off the glue. (This coat can be sprayed with aerosol paint, if desired.) For a more defined crackle finish, use a hair dryer or work in the sun.

6 Repeat step 5 with ivory paint and additional colors of paint, if desired.

7 A walnut or other wood stain can be rubbed on once paint is completely dry. Let the stain sit for 10 to 20 minutes, then rub off with a clean rag. For a more distressed look, rub moist black dirt onto planter, allow to dry, then lightly sand.

8 Apply four to five coats of polyurethane, letting dry between coats. Make sure you spray the inside and bottom of the planter as well.

9 If necessary, insert a plastic liner inside the planter or drill holes in the bottom to allow water to drain.

---

*Great
container
plants*

SUN   Aster, Clary Sage, Cosmos, Dianthus, Poppies, Jasmine, Lavender, Lemon balm, Lemon Verbena, Marigolds, Phlox, Roses (*especially miniature varieties*), Salvia, Snapdragons, Sweet peas, Verbena, and Zinnias

SHADE   Coleus, Ferns, Fuchsia, Hostas, Ivy, Impatiens, Lobelia, Pansies, Scented Geranium, Springeri, and Variegated Impatiens

EDIBLES   Blueberries, Cranberries, Cucumbers, Currants, Dwarf Cherries, Dwarf Peaches, Figs, Herbs, Lemongrass, Peppers, Pomegranate, Raspberries, Strawberries, and Tomatoes

VINE-PAINTED PLANTER

DESIGNER: **Sharon Trammel**

Another option for decorating a purchased wooden planter is to sketch a design along the sides of the planter, then fill in with paint. Stencils and clip art are useful sources of floral motifs.

Materials and Tools

Wooden planter

Exterior spray wood primer

Exterior latex semigloss paint: dark green, light green, purple (or other colors appropriate for the chosen design)

Exterior spray polyurethane

Fine sandpaper

Drawing pencil

Assorted artist paintbrushes and drawing pencils

Instructions

1 Sand the wooden planter to remove any rough edges.

2 Prime planter with exterior primer to seal the wood and to prevent knots from bleeding through the finish. Prime the inside and bottom of the planter as well. Allow primer to dry thoroughly, then lightly sand entire planter again. (Note: If the planter is redwood, you will need to use an oil-based sanding sealer [thinned oil varnish]; otherwise, a water-based primer can be used.)

3 Draw the design on the two long sides of the planter with a drawing pencil. Erase and adjust as needed until you are pleased with the design. You may want to give some thought to the plants you will be putting inside the planter, and plan the design accordingly.

4 Paint the short ends of the planter with exterior dark green paint.

5 Draw diamonds in all four corners of the top (rim) of the planter and paint the entire rim with dark and light green as shown in the photograph.

6 Paint the decorative/floral design on the long sides of the planter, using the penciled markings as a guide.

7 Apply four to five coats of polyurethane, allowing sealant to dry completely between coats. Make sure you spray the inside and bottom of the planter as well.

8 If necessary, insert a plastic liner inside the planter or drill holes in the bottom to allow water to drain.

ARTIST'S GALLERY *Gary Caldwell*

In his studio in Chapel Hill, North Carolina, Gary Caldwell creates intricate stainless steel garden sculptures that are made by drawing out the colors and textures from metal during the forging process.

LEFT: SUNFLOWER
Forged stainless steel
PHOTO: Gary Caldwell

RIGHT: TIGER BUTTERFLY
Forged stainless steel
PHOTO: Gary Caldwell

BOTTOM LEFT: BEETLE
Forged stainless steel
PHOTO: Gary Caldwell

BOTTOM RIGHT: MANTIS
Forged stainless steel
PHOTO: Gary Caldwell

CEMENT GARDEN CONTAINERS

DESIGNER: **Owen Sayles**

*M*ixing cement with readily available materials—sand, peat moss, vermiculite, and bark—and shaping the mixture into garden containers is a simple technique that yields wonderful results. These materials provide a rough, earthy appearance and encourage moss to grow, giving the pieces a wonderfully ancient look.

Materials and Supplies

Washed sand

Peat moss

Vermiculite

Finely ground bark (optional)

Type 1 cement

Cement dye (optional)

Water

Mold of your choice (see step 6 below)

Chicken wire or other reinforcing material (for containers over 10 inches [25.5 cm] wide)

Plastic for covering work surface and wrapping molds

Container for mixing

Chemical-resistant gloves

Wire brush

Instructions

1 Decide what shape and size you want your container(s) to be. Cover the work surface with plastic.

2 Place sand, peat moss, and vermiculite in a container according to the following guidelines: one to two parts sand, one part peat moss, two parts vermiculite. Add some finely ground bark to the mixture, if desired. (You will want to experiment with amounts of materials to achieve the look you want.) Work ingredients together until well mixed.

3 Add cement to mixture; use one part cement to three parts mix. If you want the container to be colored, add cement dye (available at home supply stores) at this point, according to manufacturer's instructions.

4 When all ingredients are well mixed, add water. Add water until mixture is completely wet, but not runny. If the mixture is not wet enough, materials will be brittle when the piece dries; if the mixture is too wet, the container will not hold its form.

5 Once the mixture is the correct consistency, begin forming the containers. Be sure to wear chemical-resistant gloves when picking up and forming material. If the containers are more than 10 inches (25.5 cm) wide, you will need to use chicken wire or some other reinforcement to prevent cracking and breaking.

6 You can make molds out of almost anything. This designer suggests cutting molds out of polystyrene or using plastic pots for the base molds, then using a Frisbee or a terra-cotta planter dish to make the inner space. You can also shape the inner spaces by hand (if the cement is mixed to the correct consistency). Experiment with different containers and use your imagination—finding just the right mold is half the fun. Cover the entire mold with plastic. (Plastic makes releasing the mold easier, and creates an interesting texture.)

7 Once mold is prepared, use your (glove-protected) hands to fill the base mold with cement. To make the small dishes (see below) and the simple birdbaths, either use another mold (a Frisbee or planter dish, for example) for the inner space, or shape the space by hand. To make the planter table (see page 20), you will need to make a pedestal that has been reinforced with chicken wire as well as a dish container as described in step 6. For the pedestal, use a wire brush to cup both pieces (the pedestal and the dish) so that they fit together properly.

8 Leave pots to dry thoroughly. Drying time varies, from a few hours to sometimes two or three days, depending on the size of the containers and the weather. Do not let containers dry too quickly or they will crack; wet them down periodically, if necessary.

9 Once the container is completely dry, use a wire brush to remove any loose particles.

DESIGNER: **Mardi Letson**

WEATHERED STORAGE BOX

Ever wish you had a convenient outdoor spot to stow your small garden gear? This garden storage box, an attractive addition to any garden decor, can be constructed out of weathered wood as described below; or you can distress and alter any preassembled wooden box (possibly a thrift-store find) to your liking. Mount the box on a post (a fence post or garden gatepost, for example), by the back door, or in any other spot in your garden where you frequently drop your garden gloves and hand tools.

Materials and Tools

Weathered ½-inch-thick wood board for box: two 11- x 7⅞-inch pieces for the top and bottom, two 7⅞-inch-square pieces for the sides, and one 10- x 7⅞-inch piece for the back

Weathered ⅜-inch-thick wood board: two 10½- x 8⅛-inch pieces for the shelf and the door

Wooden knob

Paint (optional)

Weathered post for mounting box (optional)

Small nails

Hammer

Router with ¼-inch (.5-cm) groove bit

Sandpaper

Instructions

1 Nail the top board (11 x 7⅞ inches) to the top of the left side board and the top of the right side board (each 7⅞ inches square) as shown in the diagram.

2 Next, nail the bottom board (11 x 7⅞ inches) and then the back board (10 x 7⅞ inches) in place.

3 Position the shelf (10½ x 8⅛ inches) in the desired location inside the box and nail through side boards to secure shelf in place.

4 Use a router to create a groove on the underside of the top board and on the front top side of the bottom board—in other words, both grooved surfaces will be on the inside of the box. These grooves serve as tracks for the door and should be positioned just inside the edge of the top and bottom pieces to allow for the door to slide in front of the left side piece and the shelf.

5 Use sandpaper to taper the top and bottom edges of the door piece to allow the door to slide smoothly in the groove.

6 Attach a knob of your choice to the door and paint the box, if necessary. (See page 17 for how to create a distressed look with paint.) Slide door into place on the front of the box.

7 Attach storage box to a weathered post or other flat surface in a convenient spot in the garden.

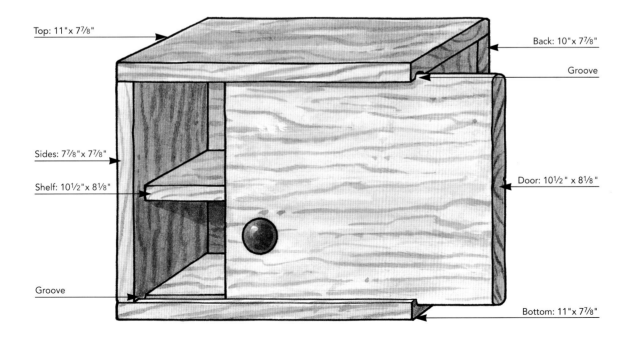

Top: 11"x 7⅞"

Back: 10"x 7⅞"

Groove

Sides: 7⅞"x 7⅞"

Shelf: 10½"x 8⅛"

Door: 10½" x 8⅛"

Groove

Bottom: 11"x 7⅞"

WIRE
GARDEN
BASKETS

These instructions are for making the large basket (left); to make the smaller (rusty) one, simply reduce the proportions. To achieve a rusty look quickly, hose down the finished piece and allow to dry outside in the sun. For the container candle holder, we've chosen an ordinary green florist's bowl, but feel free to use any glass container you have on hand.

Materials and Tools

20-gauge annealed iron wire (available at hardware stores by the spool)

Glass Christmas balls or other garden ornaments (optional)

Glass container and candle (optional)

Wire cutters

Needle-nose pliers

DESIGNER: **Skip Wade**

LARGE BASKET

Instructions

1 First you will need to construct four wire rings by forming the wire into a circle and twisting the ends back over the ring to secure. You will need one ring that is 2 inches (5 cm) in diameter, one ring that is 4 inches (10 cm) in diameter, and two rings that are 6 inches (15 cm) in diameter. (These measurements are approximate and can be varied, but keep the proportions about the same.)

2 Connect the 2-inch (5-cm) ring to the 4-inch (10-cm) ring by wrapping lengths of 12-inch (30.5-cm) wire from one ring to the other. Attach one 6-inch (15-cm) ring in the same way. These three rings form the bottom of the basket.

3 Working up from the bottom of the basket (the three attached rings), bend, loop, and twist together 12-inch (30.5-cm) lengths of wire to create the body of the basket, attaching each loop to the one before. Continue this process until the desired basket height is achieved. (The largest basket shown in the photograph [on the left] is approximately 8½ inches or 21.5 cm tall.)

4 Use 2- to 3-inch (5- to 7.5-cm) wires to attach the remaining 6-inch (15-cm) ring to the last set of loops to create the finished basket.

5 Either use the basket as is or bend and twist together three or four sets of wires in the desired length to form a hanger as we've done here. Use your imagination—bend wire into coils, curlicues, or any other shape to embellish the top (hanger) of the basket. Fill the container with glass Christmas balls or other garden ornaments.

CONTAINER CANDLE HOLDER

Instructions

1 Make two 6-inch (15-cm) wire rings as described in step 1 of the instructions for making a large basket (see left).

2 Cut three 18-inch (45.5-cm) wires and three 28-inch (71-cm) wires and wrap approximately 1 inch (2.5 cm) of each length of wire around one ring, alternating 18-inch (45.5-cm) pieces with 28-inch (71-cm) pieces.

3 Twist two adjacent wires (one of each length) together about 2 inches (5 cm) up from the ring base, then repeat with the other two pairs of wires.

4 Repeat step 3 with the next level of wire, 2 inches (5 cm) up from the last twist. Continue to twist pieces of wire together to create a chain-link-fence-like basket design in the desired height. (Place bowl in basket periodically to measure height.)

5 Next, wrap about ½ inch (1.5 cm) of each wire end around the remaining ring. Twist each of the 18-inch (45.5-cm) wires around the 28-inch (71-cm) wires until all of the 18-inch (45.5-cm) wire is used.

6 Pull the three remaining (28-inch or 71-cm) wires together, twist the ends together, then bend into a hook. (You can slide a coil of wire onto the hanger, if desired, for decoration.) Insert glass container and a candle.

IVY TOPIARY FRAME

DESIGNER: **Skip Wade**

By bending and twisting annealed wire, a simple, yet striking topiary frame can be constructed very quickly—and the structure will last for many years.

Materials and Tools

20-gauge annealed iron wire (available at hardware stores by the spool)

Glass Christmas ball or other garden ornament (optional)

Wire cutters

Needle-nose pliers

Instructions

1 Cut two 7-foot (2-m) lengths of wire and fold each piece in half to create two 42-inch (106.5-cm) lengths of double wire. Twist the two wires on each piece together.

2 Fold each piece in half again to create four twisted-wire prongs (two prongs on each piece). Stick the four prongs into the ground (or a pot) in a tipi configuration.

3 Make three rings out of twisted wire: one 4 inches (10 cm) in diameter, one 8 inches (20.5 cm) in diameter, and one 12 inches (30.5 cm) in diameter (see step 1 for large wire basket on page 25). (These measurements are approximate and can be varied, but keep the proportions about the same.)

4 Slide the 12-inch-diameter (30.5-cm) ring down over the four wires (which are now sticking up from the ground or soil). When you are about 2 inches (5 cm) from the soil, attach the large ring to the wire frame by twisting small (2- to 3-inch or 5- to 7.5-cm) wires around the joints where the ring and the wire frame meet.

5 Repeat step 4 with the 8-inch (20.5-cm) ring about halfway up the wire frame, and again with the 4-inch (10-cm) ring about 4 inches (10 cm) from the top of the frame.

6 Twist the four pieces of wire frame together at the top, leaving one wire sticking up above the frame. Place a Christmas ball or any other garden ornament on top of topiary frame. (You can bend the top of the frame to accommodate the chosen ornament.)

ARTIST'S GALLERY *Arthur Higgins*

Arthur Higgins has been a professional artist for over 36 years, and has divided much of his time and talent between fine art projects, public art commissions, and his own kinetic designs. His Wind Petal designs are unique sculptural forms that are constantly transformed as wind patterns change.

ABOVE: FLOWER & HUMMER WIND PETAL, 1998
Aluminum   PHOTO: Arthur Higgins

BELOW: FROG WIND PETAL, 1998
Brass   PHOTO: Arthur Higgins

FLUE-PIPE PLANTERS

These unusual garden containers are incredibly easy to make. First, sketch a design—either simple or complex, depending on your skill level (or mood)—around the edge of a terra-cotta flue pipe. Next, fill in the design with ceramic tiles. We've used 1-inch (2.5-cm) tiles here, but feel free to get creative with tiles in different shapes and sizes.

Materials and Tools

Terra-cotta chimney flue pipes, 8 inches (20.5-cm) square

1-inch (2.5-cm) ceramic tiles in assorted colors (with spacers)

Tile adhesive

Grout, terra-cotta or any other color of your choice

Sponge

Pencil

Craft knife

Brick or piece of wood

Tile nippers (optional)

Safety glasses (optional)

Plastic (to cover work space)

Squeegee or tile spatula

Instructions

1 Clean the surface of the terra-cotta flue pipes with a sponge and warm water. Allow to dry thoroughly.

2 Sketch the design on one edge of the flue pipe with a pencil. It is important that you do this, as the shape of the pipe, to some degree, affects the design, and you will want to adjust the design accordingly.

3 Remove the plastic spacers from between the tiles with a craft knife.

4 Lay the tiles out on a flat work surface and arrange the tiles to form the chosen design.

5 Lay your flue pipe on its side and work on one side at a time. Place a brick or a piece of wood under the flue pipe below the area where the design will go. (The pipe will be lying on its side while you apply tile.) This will protect the tiles as you turn the pipe to apply tiles to the surface.

6 Mix a small batch of tile adhesive according to the manufacturer's instructions, allowing the adhesive to cure briefly as directed. Apply adhesive to the top of the flue pipe and attach tiles to the edge of the pipe. Space tiles out with about ⅛ inch (.3 cm) or less between each tile.

7 Rotate the flue to the next side and continue applying adhesive and tiles around the entire edge of the flue pipe. You may need to break tiles to fit for the last row of tiles; you can either do this by hand or use tile nip-

pers. *Note*: Always wear safety glasses when breaking tiles with tile nippers! The adhesive will dry in approximately three to four hours, but the longer you can wait before grouting, the better.

8 Cover your work surface with plastic before grouting. Mix grout according to manufacturer's instructions and spread over tiles with a squeegee or a tile spatula. Wipe the surface until the tiles are clean, and smooth the grout channels with your finger. Use your fingers to create a smooth bottom edge. After about half an hour, use a barely damp sponge to remove grout haze from the surface. Continue wiping until clean. Allow the grout to dry overnight, and wipe the surface clean again as needed.

9 To install the planter, dig an 8-inch (20.5-cm) square hole 6 inches (15 cm) or deeper into the ground and set the pipe into the hole. Tamp dirt around pipe. Fill the pipe with a layer of large rocks, then a layer of gravel. Add dirt and plant.

Container gardening

*L*ARGE gardens take a lot of time, space, and energy, and containers are a great alternative for those who just can't tend a full-fledged garden. A wide range of plants can be grown successfully in containers: perennials (hosta, sedum, corepsis, periwinkle); bulbs (daffodils, crocus, hyacinth, tulips); annuals and biennials (forget-me-nots, daisies, pansies, candytuft, allysum); climbers (clematis, honeysuckle, jasmine, ivy); herbs (thyme, basil, rosemary, sage); fruit (fruit trees, berries); vegetables (peppers, tomatoes, lettuce, beans); and shrubs (box-wood, rhododendron, laurel). See page 17 for a list of plants that do well in containers.

Once you've decided to embark on a container garden, put some thought into where such a garden would have the biggest impact; sometimes only a few, well-placed containers are enough to transform a deck, patio, balcony, entryway, or porch. Determine the type of containers that best suit your space and style. Choose from terra-cotta, wood, ceramic, or plastic pots (in assorted sizes), metal pails and containers,

tubs, windowboxes, planters, hanging baskets, wall pots, wooden half-barrels and troughs, and stone urns and cauldrons.

Use your imagination and begin to look at old cans and discarded household items (such as sinks, tubs, and bowls) as potential decorative garden

containers. Galvanized tubs and metal buckets from hardware stores make great containers for tall plants, such as topiaries (drill holes for drainage). See page 118 for more information on using found objects in the garden.

Try positioning containers in repetitive rows on shelves or

stairways or along pathways. Large ornate pots may work best in your garden, or you may prefer to plant groupings of small traditional pots. Perch a unique pot on a pillar for a dramatic effect. Place aromatic plants at entryways, along paths or walkways, or any other spot that people will frequent.

The container will, to some degree, make a difference in the plants you will grow, or vice versa. I find it is often best to choose the style of garden you wish to create, select containers that fit your style, then consult an expert (at your local nursery) to determine which plants grow best in that particular container. Plants that are not frost resistent can be stored in containers within containers, and moved to a different location for winter storage. If you do not want to deal with moving containers, choose only hardy plants.

Ideally, containers should have holes to allow for proper drainage; you can improvise by carefully punching holes yourself, or by layering some aggregate, such as broken pieces of terra cotta, stones, or charcoal, into the bottom of the container. Remember that the smaller the pot, the more likely the soil is to dry out.

In late winter (January and February), decide which plants will go in each container, and determine whether plants should

be grown from seeds (such as nasturtium, snapdragons, marigolds, tomatoes, and salad plants) or whether seedlings should be purchased (such as petunias, impatiens, and begonias). Order all necessary seeds and seedlings. Seeds will arrive immediately, and seedlings will probably not be delivered until early or mid-spring. You may also choose to wait and buy full-grown plants.

Next, clean and repair used containers; purchase any new ones. Terra-cotta pots should be soaked before planting. Since terra-cotta is porous, it easily absorbs water from plants. When the appropriate time for planting arrives, which depends on the chosen variety, choose the most suitable soil. This decision is made much easier by consulting your local nursery. Commercially made potting soil

FACING PAGE: A metal container filled with plants in a variety of shapes and textures creates a surprisingly pleasing presentation when positioned on a rusty garden chair.
DESIGN: Christopher Mello

LEFT: Potted flowering plants can be moved easily to suit the changing needs of an outdoor space. This miniature rose bush provides a splash of color nestled among a bed of green foliage.

*Container
gardening*

LEFT: An assortment of plantings in appealing containers made from found metal objects
DESIGN: Christopher Mello

BELOW: Small terra-cotta flowerpots are covered with broken tile and pottery, then arranged on an antique nursery chair.
DESIGN: Terry Taylor

usually works fine for container gardening, and it's certainly the easiest route to go when pressed for time. (Make sure it's fresh.) However, these soil mixtures tend to be slightly too light in texture, which makes anchoring plants more difficult.

In early spring, grow daffodils or other early-blooming bulbs and sew summer-blooming annuals. As spring progresses, plant summer-blooming bulbs and more mature annuals. Once seedlings begin to emerge from the soil and grow, be sure to weed your containers regularly. Use fresh plants that are not rootbound. Make sure you position plants close together to achieve an overgrown, abundant feel. Select upright plants for central focus of the design, then fill in with creeping plants or vines that will spill over the edge of the container.

Fertilize containers every two to three weeks. This is even more important for a container garden than for an in-ground garden, since container-bound plants have access to less soil, and, thus, have less available nutrients. The smaller the container, the more feed the plants will require. You will also need to keep a close eye on which plants are due to be repotted; give these plenty of water and repot as soon as possible. Deadheading plants regularly keeps them looking fresh and encourages new growth.

PEBBLE-COVERED FLOWERPOT

This pebbled pot has the sort of handsome simplicity that makes it a nice decorative touch in a country garden—particularly when filled with a mass of informal flowers and perched on a rock wall. This pot also looks great when moss is encouraged to grow on the stones.

Materials and Tools

Pebbles (or dried beans) in assorted colors and sizes

Terra-cotta pot

Clear silicone weather-resistant adhesive

Pencil (optional)

DESIGNER: **Mardi Letson**

Instructions

1 You can either collect pebbles or buy them (usually available by the bag) at a garden or craft supply store. (Fish supply stores sometimes have a good selection as well.) Before you begin, soak pebbles in warm, soapy water to remove dirt and grit. This will not only improve the appearance of the finished pot, but will help the pebbles adhere more securely.

2 Rinse the terra-cotta pot and allow to dry thoroughly.

3 Spread pebbles out on a flat surface; this will help when choosing individual pebbles for specific spaces on the pot. If you plan to do a mosaic pot, arrange the pebbles or dried beans on your work surface and sketch the design on the pot with a pencil.

4 Working from the bottom up, attach pebbles to the exterior of the pot with adhesive. It is important to begin at the bottom; the pebbles need to be placed carefully around the bottom edge, so that the pot will sit level. When you get to the rim of the pot, position pebbles so that some extend beyond the rim.

FAUX BRONZE URN

An ordinary plaster urn (available at any garden supply store) can be turned into a splendid bronze garden ornament with the application of a few coats of paint. A variety of finishes can be achieved by using a wide range of color combinations, from dark brown to red to green to gold; simply substitute the chosen color (one that works with your garden) for the red copper color used on this urn.

Materials and Tools

Plaster urn

Spray primer/sealer, ruddy brown

Spray paint, bronze

Latex glazing liquid

Acrylic paints: red copper, burnt umber, and metallic gold

Exterior polyurethane, matte

100-grit sandpaper

Cloth rags

2-inch (5-cm) paintbrush

Instructions

1 Sand the surface of the plaster urn until all edges are smooth and any small bumps on the surface have been removed. Wipe urn clean with cloth rags.

2 Spray on a coat of ruddy brown primer to seal the plaster and allow to dry thoroughly.

3 Spray on bronze paint and allow to dry thoroughly. (Spray paint works best for the base coat, because it provides a smoother finish that best imitates a metal finish.)

4 Mix 2 tablespoons glazing liquid with 1 tablespoon water and 1 tablespoon red copper acrylic paint. Brush the red glaze on heavily and use the tip of the brush to stipple the glaze into the recesses of the urn. Lightly wipe urn with a clean rag in a streaky motion, leaving more paint in some areas than others.

5 Using the same method as described in step 4, mix a burnt umber glaze (glazing liquid, water, and burnt umber paint), and apply to the urn. Make sure to leave this darker glaze in the crevices. Allow to dry thoroughly.

6 Mix 1 tablespoon of metallic gold acrylic paint into the burnt umber glaze to a achieve a warm bronze tone. Apply this color to the urn as described in step 4 above. Allow to dry thoroughly.

7 Spray four to five coats of exterior polyurethane in a matte finish; let dry between coats.

GARDENER'S TIP *A coat of gray- or rust-colored flat paint or primer can give a new planter or decorative garden element an instant ancient appearance*

the
Well-Decorated
GARDEN
Chapter 2

Stakes &
Markers

TWISTED WIRE STAKES

*C*opper wire can be twisted into any shape to make tops for these whimsical garden stakes. Use them to draw attention to your favorite plants or to perk up areas of the garden that need extra pizzazz.

Materials and Tools

Copper wire: 12-gauge for both stakes and 6-gauge for the moon stake

Wooden dowel rod in any size

Small wire brads

Flat-nose pliers

Hammer

STAR STAKE

Instructions

1 Coil one end of 12-gauge copper wire with flat-nose pliers. *Note*: the length of wire you need will vary, depending on how large you want your designs to be.

2 Start a brad about 4 inches (10 cm) down from one end of the dowel rod by holding the brad with pliers and tapping it partially into the dowel with a hammer.

3 Hold the coil against the dowel next to the brad, then hammer the brad over the wire to secure as shown in the photograph (best seen on the moon stake).

4 Wrap the wire up around the end of the dowel, using brads to tack the wire in place as you work.

5 When you get to the top of the dowel, use a brad to tack the wire in place in the center of the dowel, then bend the wire upward. You can tighten the wire against the dowel by pinching the wire end with the flat-nose pliers and turning. Twist the wire around several times in this manner, always turning the pliers in the same direction.

6 Once you have created a base that is about 2 inches (5 cm) from the top of the dowel, begin to shape the wire into a star. You may want to use pliers to form neat corners.

7 Continue to wrap wire around the star until you are pleased with the shape and appearance, then wind the wire back down to the dowel. Trim end of wire.

DESIGNER:
Melanie Woodson

MOON STAKE

Instructions

1 Using 6-gauge wire, form the shape of a crescent moon with a face profile. Use the photograph as a guide.

2 Coil one end of 12-gauge wire and tack it to the dowel with a brad about 3 inches (7.5 cm) from one end of the dowel (see step 3 in the star stake instructions).

3 Wrap the wire up around the dowel and tack the wire to the top of the dowel with a brad (see step 5 in the star stake instructions). Begin twisting the 12-gauge wire around the moon shape about 3 inches (7.5 cm) from the top of the dowel. This will be a little difficult the first time around, but will get easier.

4 Keep twisting the wire until you are pleased with the shape and appearance of the moon. Twist the wire back down to the dowel rod and trim end of wire.

ELEGANT PLANT MARKERS

Dress up your garden with these exquisite plant markers. Since the paper labels are sealed tightly inside glass, you can create identifiers that are as elaborate as you wish—try miniature watercolors. Don't forget that copper wire will turn green with outdoor exposure; if you'd rather keep your markers copper-colored, spray them with a coat of sealant.

Materials and Tools (for one plant marker)

Heavy-duty wire coat hanger

5 feet (1.5 m) solid copper wire (see step 2)

2-inch (5-cm) square paper label (see step 4)

100% silicone glue

Single weight glass, 3 inches (7.5 cm) square

Beveled glass, 3 inches (7.5 cm) square

13 inches (33 cm) ⅜-inch (1-cm) copper foil tape (available at stained-glass suppliers)

Copper wire loop, or 1½-inch (4-cm) piece of fine-gauge copper wire

Copper tinting (available at stained-glass suppliers)

Spray lacquer or polyurethane (optional)

Wire cutters

Craft knife

Small paintbrush

Soldering gun

DESIGNER: **Kim Tibbals-Thompson**

Instructions

1 Use wire cutters to cut coat hanger 3½ inches (9 cm) in from the bottom angles on each side, and bend in each short side so that it is parallel with the bottom (long) side. On one short side, bend up about one inch (2.5 cm) to form a hook; this will be at the top of the plant marker.

2 Solid copper wire is available plastic coated in the electrical section of hardware stores. Strip plastic coating from the copper wire with a craft knife by holding the knife nearly parallel with wire, cutting into plastic, and pulling wire through blade.

3 Coil one end of the copper wire into a ½-inch (1.5-cm) flat coil; the coil will hide the raw coat-hanger tip on the hook. Position coil over tip and begin wrapping, twisting, and looping the copper wire around the coat hanger. No large wire loops should fall more than 4 inches (10 cm) from the bottom of the coat hanger. Trim excess wire.

4 You can either use computer-generated labels (clip art), hand-letter your own labels, or use the template we've provided. Apply a small amount of 100% silicone glue to the back of each corner of the paper label, and adhere label to the center of the square of single-weight glass. Place the square of beveled glass on top, sandwiching the label between the glass pieces. Use a small paintbrush to lightly seal the edges of the glass pieces with silicone glue.

5 Adhere copper foil tape to the edges of the glass, centering on the seam where the two pieces of glass meet. Wrap foil around all four sides and burnish down the outer edges of the tape onto each side of the glass pieces to assure good contact. Overlap foil tape by ⅛ to ¼ inch (.3 to .5 cm) where ends of tape meet.

6 Apply solder to all surfaces of the copper foil tape and solder copper loop to the top of the corner.

7 Apply copper tinting to soldering to give the edges a copper color. If you do not want the markers to turn green with age (verdigris), apply a coat of spray lacquer or polyurethane to the copper surfaces.

ENLARGE 200%.

RUSTIC PLANT MARKERS

I dentify your plants while adding decorative flair to your garden beds and potted flowers. These adorable markers, made with twigs and vine gathered from a walk in the woods, are a splendid alternative to ordinary metal plant markers.

DESIGNER:
Mardi Letson

GARDENER'S TIP *Use found decorative objects, such as interesting rocks and pebbles, shells, and single ceramic tiles, to embellish and personalize your garden space.*

Materials and Tools

Small pieces of thin wood board, cut to the desired size (see step 1)

Miniature 3-inch (7.5-cm) grapevine wreaths or small twigs (approximately ¼ inch [.5 cm] in diameter)

Clear silicone weather-resistant adhesive

Small nails (optional)

Exterior polyurethane

Permanent black marker

Small garden pruners

Small paintbrush

Instructions

1 Use a permanent marker to neatly write plant names on pieces of wood board. *Note:* these markers use wood pieces in the following dimensions: 2¼ x 1⅛ inches (5.5 x 2.8 cm) for the wreath markers and 4¼ x ⅞ inches (11 x 2.2 cm) for the twig-framed markers.

2 To make the wreath marker, nestle a piece of wood board into the center of the grapevine wreath and secure board in place with clear silicone weather-resistant adhesive. You can shape pieces of grapevine to make your own wreaths; they are also widely available (and quite inexpensive) at craft supply stores. To make the twig-framed markers, use pruners to cut twigs to the lengths needed to frame board and secure twigs to board with adhesive.

3 Stakes can either be an extension of the framing (as with the *lavandula* and *pelargonium* markers shown in the photographs), or can be added (to both styles) by attaching a twig to the back of the marker with adhesive and/or a small nail.

4 When the adhesive is completely dry, use a small paintbrush to coat each marker entirely (including the ends of the twigs) with exterior polyurethane.

ABOVE: CHICKEN AND TURTLE, 1998
Galvanized steel wire. PHOTO: Evan Bracken

BELOW: SNAKE, 1998
Galvanized steel wire. PHOTO: Evan Bracken

Garden edging

*E*DGING keeps grass from entering flower beds and gives the garden a neat, clean look. In addition, carefully planned edging can add a decorative element to the garden, whether you choose an elegant wrought-iron Victorian border that keeps kids and animals (as well as grass) at bay or a row of crumbling (albeit charming) bricks.

Commercially made edging is available in an array of materials, such as concrete, stone, terra cotta, and metal, and varies widely in price. Plastic edging is commonly found in home centers and garden supply stores, though it is not advisable to use it, as changes in ground temperature will cause the plastic to heave out of the ground.

Metal edging is relatively inexpensive, widely available, and among the easiest type of edging to install. For gardeners who do not want edging to be visible, metal is probably the best choice. Railroad ties work well for linear flower beds. Stone edging will last a long time, though this tends to be the most expensive type of edging. Some gardeners collect stones on their property, which cuts costs considerably.

If you can't afford to purchase edging or if you prefer to use materials with a bit more character and originality, all you need is a healthy imagination and a willingness to seek out found objects that make nice edging. Among the best choices are recrete (broken pieces of concrete), glass bottles, brick, corrugated metal, landscape timbers, and stones. A pleasing jagged edge can be easily created by edging a flower bed with bricks set at an angle—these are called

soldier bricks. At his studio garden, ceramicist Mark Burleson displays discarded pieces of handmade ceramic along his simple stone edging to create a unique border element (see photograph above). The path is made from shards of terra cotta he found nearby. (See page 112 for information on creating garden paths and walkways.)

In most cases, installation is as easy as inserting the edging pieces into the ground. Before you begin to install edging, position a hose in the configuration you have chosen to use as a guide. (Edging with smooth, round lines is much easier to install and will make mowing easier.) Most edging can be pressed into the soil by hand or with a little help from a rubber mallet. Stone pieces will need to have a trench dug to a depth of about half the stone. Once the stone is placed in the trench, tamp the soil around the stone until the edging is set firmly in place.

TILE GARDEN PLAQUES

These simple tile stakes are incredibly easy to put together, but have quite an impact when placed strategically throughout the garden. They can be used as edging or borders, or try labeling solid-colored ceramic tiles with a permanent marker to identify your herbs, flowers, and vegetables.

Materials and Tools

Assorted ceramic tiles

Wooden paint sticks

Spray paint

Ceramic tile adhesive

Instructions

1 Choose tiles in colors and shapes that complement the color scheme of your garden. This project is a great way to make use of leftover tiles; it is also possible to buy individual tiles from ceramic tile suppliers for very little money.

2 Spray-paint the wooden paint sticks with a color that complements your chosen tiles. (Paint sticks are available at any paint store.) Allow paint to dry thoroughly.

3 Apply ceramic tile adhesive to the back of the tile and attach paint stick. Make sure you use a thick layer of adhesive for a secure bond. The stick should be attached along the entire length of the tile to give the decoration the optimum stability when placed in the ground. Allow tile adhesive to dry for at least 24 hours.

4 Spray-paint the back of the tile with the same color paint as you used for the stick; make sure adhesive is completely covered with paint. Allow paint to dry thoroughly.

DESIGNER: **Tamara Miller**

the
Well-Decorated
GARDEN

STAINED GLASS CHIMES STAKE

A garden stake made with shards of colorful stained glass and copper wire will not only support your favorite rose topiary, but will shimmer against the morning light and chime pleasantly in the wind. Try topping stakes with antique doorknobs, finials, painted wooden pulls, beads, and large marbles.

GARDENER'S TIP *To give a new terra-cotta pot a weathered look, apply a coat of yogurt to the surface of the pot with a paintbrush, then leave pot outdoors to dry for several weeks.*

DESIGNER: **Melanie Woodson**

44

Materials and Tools

4 pieces of stained glass.
(Most stained glass
shops sell scrap glass.)

12-gauge copper wire

3 heavy-gauge copper rings.
(You can purchase these
or make your own by
wrapping heavy-gauge
copper wire around
something round.)

Wooden dowel rod, ¾ to
1 inch (2 to 2.5 cm) wide

1-inch (2.5-cm) square
of copper sheeting

Flat-nose pliers

Electric drill

Hammer

Instructions

1 Determine which piece of glass you would like to be on top of the stake (perhaps the most striking or nicely shaped piece), then wrap 12-gauge copper wire around the chosen piece as tightly as possible. Twist and shape the wire into an interesting pattern as you wrap (refer to the photograph below).

2 Once you have wrapped the entire piece of top glass, twist the two wire ends together tightly; you will need to leave a few inches (5 cm) of twisted wire at the bottom of the piece of glass (see photograph). Next, use flat-nose pliers to tighten the wire by pinching the wire with the pliers and making a quar-

ter turn to the right. Do this in several places on the wire until it feels secure and you are pleased with how it looks.

3 Wrap the other three pieces of glass with wire, using the same technique as described in steps 1 and 2. You will not need quite as much extra wire on the ends of these glass pieces. Once all the hanging glass pieces are wrapped with wire, bend the twisted wire on each piece around a copper ring. Cut off extra wire.

4 Cut three 5-inch (12.5-cm) pieces of wire, and coil one end of each piece (see photograph).

5 Drill a hole in the center of one end of the dowel rod, about 2 inches (5 cm) deep, using a bit the same thickness as the diameter of the twisted wire portion (on the bottom—see step 2) of the top glass piece and the three coiled wire pieces when held together. Use the same bit to drill a hole in the square of copper sheeting.

6 Put the top glass piece and the three wire pieces through the hole in the sheeting, then into the hole in the dowel as far as it will go. Next, hold the sheeting in place on top of the dowel and bang the sheeting against the sides of the dowel with the hammer.

7 To attach the hanging glass pieces, bend each coiled wire around a copper ring (see photograph) and arrange pieces around the center glass piece.

FLOWERPOT STAKES

Garden stakes double as raised flower containers and add extra blooms to the garden. Here, we've provided two variations—use your imagination to create your own elevated container garden.

DESIGNER: **Melanie Woodson**

SINGLE FLOWERPOT STAKE

Materials and Tools

Dowel rod, 1 inch (2.5 cm)
in diameter

24 inches (61 cm) 12-gauge
(or thicker) copper wire

Several small wire brads

3-inch (7.5-cm) wide copper disc
or washer

1-inch (2.5-cm) square piece
of metal sheeting

2-inch (5-cm) nail

Small terra-cotta flowerpot

Saw (if dowel ends need to be cut)

Wire cutters

Electric drill

Flat-nose or chain-nose pliers

Hammer

Nail set (nail punch)

Instructions

1 Cut a piece of 1-inch-diameter (2.5-cm) dowel rod to the desired height. (The height will vary, depending on where the stake will go and what needs to be staked.)

2 Cut four pieces of thick copper wire, each to about 6 inches (15 cm) in length.

3 Drill a hole in the center of the dowel on one end, using a drill bit that is a little wider than the diameter of the four wire pieces when held together. The drilled hole should be about 2 inches (5 cm) deep.

4 Coil one end of each wire piece. Place the other end of the wires into the hole in the dowel. Bend the wires down, flattening them against the top of the dowel, then against the sides. Hold the wires around the dowel firmly with one hand while you hammer to flatten the wires against the dowel. You can hammer around the sides as well to help bend the wires.

5 Hold a small brad with flat-nose pliers, about ½ inch (1.5 cm) from the top of the dowel rod, and begin to tack the brad into the side of the dowel. Hold one wire to the right of the brad and hammer the brad to the left and around the wire to hold it in place. Work your way around the dowel, tacking each wire piece in the same way. Make sure you space the wires evenly.

6 This step is very similar to step 5. Start a brad in about an inch (2.5 cm) lower than the brads you have already hammered in place. Hold a piece of wire from the lower brad on the right against the left side of the brad you just started, and hammer the brad to the right and around the wire. Repeat this step for all four wires.

7 Continue to create the wire design along the dowel by bending each wire to the right again and pulling against the brads. Make a bend to the left in each wire with flat-nose pliers. Use the hammer to flatten the wires out.

8 If you are using a copper disc, you will need to make a hole in the center, using a drill or a hammer and nail. If you are using a washer, skip this step.

9 To attach the pot to the dowel base, you may need a friend to help hold everything in place while you hammer. Start the 2-inch (5-cm) nail into the center of the 1-inch (2.5-cm) square of copper sheeting. Hold the dowel upright, with the hole in the disc or washer lined up with the hole in the dowel (where the wires go in).

10 Line up the hole in the bottom of the pot with the other two holes. When you get everything lined up, place the nail set on the nail head, and hammer the nail into the dowel. (A nail set [also called a nail punch] is an extension that is placed on the nail head when it is difficult for a hammer to get into a space; in this case, the pot makes it difficult to hammer in the nail.) The 2-inch (5-cm) nail should be nailed into the center of the four wires. The nail will go through the holes in the pot and the sheeting and hold the pot on the dowel rod. Plant the flowerpot.

DESIGNER: **Melanie Woodson**

HANGING FLOWERPOTS STAKE

Materials and Tools

60 inches (150 cm) 12-gauge
    copper wire

24 inches (61 cm) 6-gauge
    copper wire

2 small terra-cotta flowerpots

Two heavy-gauge copper rings

1-inch (2.5-cm) dowel rod

Small piece of copper sheeting
    (to fit over end of dowel)

Wire cutters

Pencil

Flat-nose and round-nose pliers

Electric drill and bit

Instructions

1 Cut four pieces of 12-gauge wire into 15-inch (38-cm) lengths. Mark the middle of each wire with a pencil.

2 Hold two of the wires on either side of one flowerpot (one on each side), lining up the middle of the wires with the middle of the side of the pot just under the lip. Hold wires tightly with one hand while you twist the wire ends together on one side of the pot with flat-nose pliers. Twist as evenly as possible all the way to the end of the wires.

3 Repeat this process on the other side of the pot with the other two wire ends. It will be easier for this side, because after a few twists, the wire will stay in place. You want the wire to be tight just under the lip of the flowerpot as shown in the photograph above. Make sure the wire ends are even on each side of the pot; you may need to trim the wire edges.

4 Bend each end of twisted wire into a small loop with round-nose pliers, then bend each end again into a larger loop as shown in the photograph.

5 Repeat the steps 1 though 4 with the other pot and the other two wires.

6 Attach a heavy-gauge copper ring to each flowerpot by looping the wire ends around the ring and squeezing the loops together with your fingers.

7 To make the stake holder, cut two pieces of 6-gauge wire to 12 inches (30.5 cm) each. Hold the pieces of wire together with round-nose pliers about 4 inches (10 cm) from the end.

8 Using flat-nose pliers, twist the wires together evenly all the way to the end of the wire. Trim off excess wire, making sure the ends are even. Make a small loop, then a larger loop on each of the untwisted ends with round-nose pliers.

9 Using your hands and pliers if necessary, bend each wire into an arch with the double loops opposite each other.

10 Using a drill bit about the same size as the twisted end of the 6-gauge wires, drill a hole in the center of one end of the dowel about 2 inches (5 cm) deep. Drill a hole the same size in the piece of copper sheeting.

11 Pull the twisted end of the 6-gauge wires through the sheeting, then twist the wires into the dowel as far as they will go. Pull the sheeting as close to the dowel as possible, then hammer the edges of the sheeting down around the dowel.

12 Plant the pots, then hang pots on the wire loops.

Sandy Stragnell

Sandy Stragnell, inspired by the nature of the Adirondack region of New York, creates unique metal sculptures from recycled copper, brass, and steel. He says his art "reflects [his] belief in the circle of life and the need to recycle and reuse all that we can."

BUTTERFLIES, 1992, Recycled copper   PHOTO: Marguerite Fredrick

A PELICAN WAITS, 1995
Recycled steel parts, recycled cultivator tine, brass rod   PHOTO: Marguerite Fredrick

the
Well-Decorated
GARDEN

Chapter 3

Garden
Wildlife

BUTTERFLY BOX

Attract butterflies to the garden and provide them with shelter for hibernation or resting with this handsome and easy-to-construct house.

Materials and Tools

¾-inch-thick wood: 1 piece 5 x 20 inches and 1 piece 3½ x 40 inches

Twelve 1¼-inch (3-cm) coarse-thread screws

Exterior latex paint: forest green and yellow

Saw

Protractor

Screwdriver

Electric drill with ⅛-inch (.3-cm) and ½-inch (1.5-cm) bits

Wood file

Router with ¼-inch (.5-cm) round-over bit and ½-inch (1.5-cm) straight bit (optional) or fine sandpaper

Small paintbrush

Instructions

1 From the 5-inch-wide board, cut the roof piece 7 inches long and the back piece 12¾ inches long.

2 With a protractor, measure and mark a 15° degree angle at one narrow end of the back piece and one long edge of the roof. Cut bevels in these pieces.

3 Mark the two front corners of the roof piece, opposite the beveled edge, 1 inch along each side, draw a line to connect marks, then cut off the corners. Round over all sides except the beveled sides with a router or sandpaper.

4 From the 3½-inch-wide wood stock, cut the front (door) piece 11½ inches long, bevel the top edge at a 15° angle, and round over all other edges. On the front of this piece, draw a line down the center. Mark points at 2 inches, 5 inches, 7 inches, and 10 inches. If you have a router, route a ½-inch slot between the 2-inch and 5-inch marks and between the 7-inch and 10-inch marks. If not, use an electric drill to make connecting holes between these points, then even the slot up using a wood file. Round over the slots.

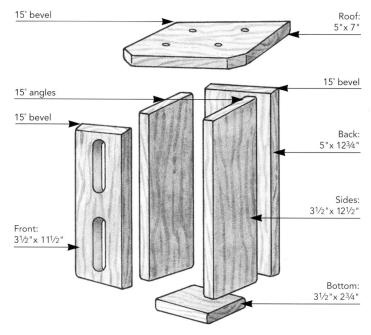

15° bevel

Roof: 5" x 7"

15° angles

15° bevel

15° bevel

Back: 5" x 12¾"

Sides: 3½" x 12½"

Front: 3½" x 11½"

Bottom: 3½" x 2¾"

GARDENER'S TIP *Every spectacular butterfly was once a caterpillar, so keeping caterpillars happy will increase the likelihood that butterflies will frequent your garden. Caterpillars feed on the foliage of plants and trees. They are especially fond of milkweed, hibiscus, parsley, beans, and a variety of other vegetables. Be aware, though, that caterpillars may leave chew marks on the leaves or stems of these plants.*

DESIGNER: **Robin Clark**

5 From the 3½-inch wood stock, cut the bottom (floor) piece to 3½ inches, then rip it to 2¾ inches wide; round over one long side and both edges.

6 From the 3½-inch wood stock, cut two side pieces 12½ inches long with a 15° angle towards the front edge (which should be about 11½ inches long after the angle is cut). Round over the front and bottom edges. Drill a pilot hole ⅜ inch (1 cm) in from the edge, 1 inch (2.5 cm) down from the angle on the front edge, and another one centered along the bottom.

7 Use screws for all assembly. Attach the sides to the back using two screws per side, keeping the top of the sides flush with the angled top of the back.

8 Attach the door to the sides with two screws, again keeping the beveled door flush with the angled sides. Insert the floor flush with the bottom of the sides and screw into position.

9 Position the roof so the beveled edge is flush with the back and it overlaps equally both sides. Secure with two screws on each side.

10 Round over the exposed edges of the back. Drill two mounting holes in the back, if desired.

11 To finish, first sand smooth all surfaces. Paint the roof forest green, allow to dry, then paint the rest of the butterfly box yellow.

VICTORIAN BIRD FEEDER

This charming bird feeder, situated in a pleasant setting among spikes of lavender, yellow yarrow, coneflowers, and a host of other colorful blooms, is guaranteed to attract feathered friends from miles away.

Materials and Tools

¾-inch-thick wood: two 18- x 5½-inch pieces for sides and one 23⅝- x 5½-inch piece for the bottom

⅜-inch-thick wood slats or trim: two 22⅛- x 1½-inch pieces

Five #8 1½-inch (4-cm) screws

Finishing nails

1 prefinished decorative wood trim (for bottom)

1 prefinished gingerbread trim piece with a right angle (Approximately 7 x 7 x 10 inches)

4-inch-long (10-cm) ¼-inch (.5-cm) screw eye with locking acorn nut

White spray lacquer

Water sealant finish

Sandpaper

Saw

Miter box with 45° angle setting

Screwdriver

Hammer

Wood glue

Electric drill

Instructions

1 Use a saw and a miter box to cut short ends of pieces of wood and wood slats to the 45° angles. Lightly sand rough-cut edges.

2 Referring to the diagram below, put side A and side B together at 45° ends to form a right angle; carefully align edges, then secure with four screws—two screws from side A into side B and two from side B into side A. Do not screw into the direct center of the two boards; you will need this area to attach the screw eye to hang the feeder.

3 With the sides of the feeder secured, the bottom board should slip exactly into place to form a triangle (see diagram). Using finishing nails (nailed from the sides into the bottom), attach the bottom board to the feeder. (Apply wood glue along edges before nailing.)

4 Glue wood slat or trim pieces on top of the bottom pieces flush with outer edges, then secure with finishing nails (which are nailed from the bottom of the feeder up through the wood slats).

5 Attach decorative trim to the bottom of the feeder with a screw.

6 Using wood glue and finishing nails, attach right-angle trim pieces to the inside right angle of the feeder in the direct center.

7 Drill a hole for the screw eye from the center upper edge of the triangle through the right-angle trim piece. Insert screw eye and attach locking acorn.

8 To finish bird feeder, first apply three coats of white spray paint, then apply polyurethane to protect from moisture.

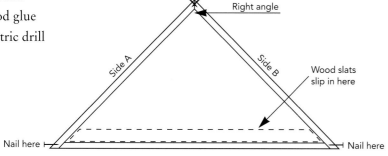

DESIGNER: **Kim Tibbals-Thompson**

SIGN BIRD FEEDER

Discarded signs and license plates can be purchased at flea markets, yard sales, and thrift shops. And they make terrific garden decorations—even when simply nailed to the door of a rustic shed. Here, we've adorned the roof of a purchased bird feeder with a colorful "detour" sign and constructed small sign reproductions to use as decorative accents.

Materials and Tools

Preassembled bird feeder
    with A-line roof

Road signs or license plates

Small pieces of wood cut to the
    shape of assorted road signs

Acrylic paint

2 small screw eyes

Length of chain

Nails or screws

Wood glue

Electric drill

Instructions

1 Choose a preassembled bird feeder that has a definite A-line roof. This style is commonly found at garden and building supply stores, and works best for use with rectangular signs or license plates that can be bent easily in the middle.

2 Secure the chosen sign or license plate to the bird feeder with nails or screws. (If you are using license plates, you may need to put one plate on each side of the feeder.)

3 To make miniature signs for the front and back of the bird feeder, freehand sign designs on the precut wood pieces with acrylic paints in the appropriate colors. Attach decorative miniature signs to the front and back of feeder with wood glue.

4 Drill two holes in the top of the feeder and insert screw eyes into holes. Glue each end of the length of chain to a screw eye to make a hanger. Hang feeder at your favorite bird intersection.

DESIGNER: **Tamara Miller**

Attracting birds

WHO among us can resist the pleasant chirping of birds in the morning or the whimsical fluttering of a feathered guest in a birdbath? There is no question that gardens are better places when birds are among its visitors. Here are some tips to help you beckon birds to your garden.

Provide birds with shelter, food, and water, and you're sure to get more than a few visitors. You should do some research and decide which types of birds you wish to attract, then choose a birdhouse, or nesting house, that is well suited (has the proper dimensions and appropriately sized entrance holes) for your chosen birds. Do similar research into the proper location for the house (how far above the ground, and so forth). Purple martins, for example, like abodes that are high above the ground and have multiple compartments. Your local extension agency, nursery, or nature center will be able to help you determine which birds are most likely to visit your area and what you will need to do to increase the chances that they will come to your garden.

A variety of birdhouses abound in garden supply stores everywhere, but some birds, such as cardinals or the Carolina wren, do not nest in houses, but prefer a pile of brush, an overgrown area, a patch of wildflowers, or an uncut section of the backyard. Leaving out a container filled with potential nest-building materials is a great way to encourage birds to nest nearby; try an assortment of fabric scraps, twigs, wool, feathers, bark, moss, and paper. Make sure you keep the strips of materials less than 4 inches (10 cm) in length.

Fill bird feeders with food that appeals to the bird varieties you want to attract. Warblers, woodpeckers, chickadees, and thrushes enjoy suet feeders. Insects are a favorite food for birds, so consider planting flowers and herbs that attract insects, such as nasturtium, fennel, parsley, thyme, and yarrow. Compost piles are a source of insects for birds as well. Berry-rich or seed-filled bushes, shrubs, flowers, or vines are also favorites. Winged visitors are especially fond of honeysuckle, vetch, burning bush, clover, juniper, holly, aster, sunflowers, snowberry, goldenrod, marigolds, salvia, sedum, and zinnias. Pine, spruce, hemlock, birch, elm, maple, mountain ash, dogwood, and cherry trees provide cones, nectar, and seeds for birds (not to mention shelter).

A fresh source of water is essential in attracting feathered guests to the garden, whether it be a natural water source (a lake or pond, for example), a birdbath, or any other place where water can collect. A birdbath will surely entice a bird or two year-round. The wide variety of commercially made birdbaths available is a testament to the value they add to the garden—both decorative and functional. However, it's just as easy to fill a strategically positioned bucket or bowl with water—and birds like it just as well. Be sure to refresh the water periodically and to keep the birdbath clean.

Some birdbath basics: Water should never be more than 2½ inches (6.5 cm) deep, and the container should slope from the edges to the center so that different-sized birds can wade in to a comfortable depth. Birds like birdbaths with a bottom surface that is slightly rough. And since they are most vulnerable when they are wet, birds prefer to bathe in a spot with good visibility. Also, the bath should be placed away from any bird feeders and birdhouses.

ARTISTS GALLERY

David Rogers

David H.G. Rogers started sculpting large, abstract outdoor sculptures with welded steel and salvaged materials at the age of 13. Over the past 25 years, Rogers has used a variety of materials and techniques to create garden sculptures. Most recently, he uses found natural materials, especially wood.

PRAYING MANTIS (BIG BUGS EXHIBIT), 1995
Black locust wood   PHOTO: Harry Grod

BUTTERFLY (BIG BUGS FOREVER), 1998
Black walnut and plate fungi   PHOTO: Harry Grod

RUSTIC STONE BIRDHOUSE

T*his handsome rock cabin in miniature provides lofty shelter for a variety of birds and is a unique decorative element for the garden.*

Materials and Tools

A-frame-style wooden birdhouse

2 x 2 pine board (actual dimensions are 1½ x 1½ inches)

Waterproof exterior-grade adhesive

Assorted small stones

2 rough-cut ½- x 8-inch boards (for roof and base)

Sheet moss

Assorted pieces of green smoke vine, or any other flexible vine, such as grapevine, laurel, or bittersweet

Electric drill with 1⅛-inch (2.8-cm) and 1¼-inch (3-cm) drill bits (optional)

Hammer

Nails

Miter box

Hot-glue gun

Instructions

1 Build or buy an A-frame-style wooden birdhouse. They're available at garden supply stores and home centers. If there isn't already a hole in the birdhouse, drill one about half the way down on the front of the house.

2 The 2 x 2 pine board will be the chimney; nail the board to the backside of the birdhouse (see photograph for placement).

3 Apply a thin coat of waterproof exterior-grade adhesive to the front, sides, and chimney of the house and press rocks into adhesive (see photograph).

4 Cut one ½- x 8-inch (1.5- x 20.5-cm) board in half and miter one edge of each piece to a 45° angle. Construct a simple roof by nailing these pieces to the top of the birdhouse, with the angled pieces at the top. Layer sheet moss on top of the roof and secure moss with hot glue.

5 Nail thick pieces of smoke vine (or other flexible vine) to the front edges of the roof as shown in the photograph. Randomly nail smaller pieces of smoke vine to the rooftop to help hold the moss in place and for added visual interest.

6 Use the remaining ½- x 8-inch (1.5- x 20.5-cm) board as the base of the birdhouse. Attach moss and smoke vine to the base as you did for the rooftop (see step 5).

7 Nail a twisted piece of smoke vine to the top of the house to form a handle.

DESIGNER: **Bobby Howard**
FOR APPLEWOOD CRAFTS (ASHEVILLE, NORTH CAROLINA)

PAINTED GOURD BIRDHOUSES

DESIGNER: **Gladys Smith**

Attract feathered guests to your garden by hanging these delightful painted gourds. Either find simple floral designs (in garden books and magazines) and transfer them to the gourds or freehand your own favorite flowers.

Materials and Tools
(for one birdhouse)

Dried gourd, approximately
    9 inches (23 cm) in diameter

¼ cup (60 ml) bleach

1 gallon (3.8 l) water

1 yard (.9 m) twine

Exterior latex wood primer,
    white (optional)

Exterior latex paint, white
    (optional)

Acrylic artist paints

High-gloss spar urethane spray

Rubber gloves

Pot scrubber or steel wool pad

Drill or sharp knife

Pencil

Dust mask (optional)

Clean sponge

Tracing paper (optional)

Assorted paintbrushes

Instructions

1 Soak the gourd in a solution of ¼ cup (60 ml) bleach to a gallon (3.8 l) of water for half an hour. Wearing rubber gloves, scrub the gourd with a pot scrubber or a steel wool pad. Take care to remove every bit of dirt, mold, and mildew from the gourd; otherwise, the paint will eventually flake off. Rinse, towel dry, then air dry for at least half an hour.

2 To allow for hanging, drill or carve a ⁵⁄₁₆-inch (.5 cm) hole through both sides of the gourd about 1 inch (2.5 cm) down from the top (see photograph). Make a hanger out of twine and attach to gourd through holes.

3 Hang the gourd to find the best position for the entry hole and mark with a pencil 4 to 6 inches (10 to 15 cm) above the gourd bottom. A 1½-inch (4-cm) diameter opening will attract a wide variety of birds, such as wrens, chickadees, nuthatches, and tree swallows. Use a drill or a sharp utility knife to make the opening.

4 Completely clean out the inside of the gourd. (Wearing a dust mask will keep the dried pulp dust out of your mouth.)

5 If you do not want a painted background, skip to step 6. If you would like the gourd to have a white background, dab on outdoor primer with a sponge. Hang gourd and allow to dry thoroughly. Sponge on one to two coats of white exterior latex paint over the primer. Paint all cut edges, but be sure no paint gets inside the gourd and keep holes free of clogs. Hang gourd and allow to dry thoroughly.

6 Pencil the chosen design onto the surface of the gourd. Either transfer the design with tracing paper or freehand the design directly onto the gourd.

7 Use assorted paintbrushes to fill in the design with acrylic paint. Erase all tracing lines when the paint has thoroughly dried.

8 Hang gourd and spray with a coat of high-gloss spar urethane, again taking care not to clog the holes or allow finish inside the gourd.

ARTIST'S GALLERY

Cyr William Smith

Cyr William Smith combines his artistic abilities with his appreciation for the natural world to create his functional handmade garden sculptures. When Smith's creations are fully operational (as garden sprinklers), dancing patterns of water carry his artistic visions into the surrounding garden.

PHOTOS TOP AND BOTTOM: GARDEN ART SPRINKLERS
Brass, copper, glass   PHOTOS: Cyr W. Smith

LADYBUG COTTAGE

L adybugs are said to be the gardener's best friend, because they help control garden pests, and can eat up to 100 aphids a day! This charming cottage is designed to attract these benevolent insects. You can buy live ladybugs and ladybug lures in the spring from garden supply centers, or collect ladybugs yourself and store them in your refrigerator over the winter (see Gardener's Tip on page 61).

Materials and Tools

¾-inch-thick wood: 1 piece 5 x 14 inches and 1 piece 3½ x 24 inches

Twelve 1¼-inch (3-cm) coarse-thread screws

Exterior latex paint: sky blue and yellow

Saw

Protractor

Screwdriver

Electric drill with ⅛-inch (.3-cm) bit

Router with ¼-inch (.5-cm) round-over bit (optional) or fine sandpaper

Small paintbrush

Instructions

1 Cut two 7-inch-long pieces from the 5-inch-wide wood board. With a protractor, measure and mark a 15° angle on the short end of one piece (for the back) and the long edge of the other piece (for the roof). Cut bevels in these pieces.

2 Mark the two front corners of the roof piece, opposite the beveled edge, 1 inch along each side, draw a line to connect marks, then cut off the corners. Round over all sides except the beveled sides with a router or sandpaper.

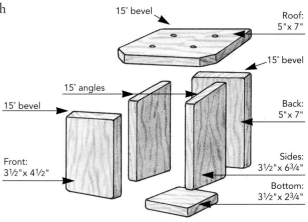

15° bevel

Roof: 5" x 7"

15° bevel

15° angles

15° bevel

Back: 5" x 7"

Front: 3½" x 4½"

Sides: 3½" x 6¾"

Bottom: 3½" x 2¾"

3 From the 3½-inch-wide wood stock, cut the front (door) piece 4¼ inches long, bevel the top edge to a 15° angle, and round over all other edges. Cut the bottom (floor) 3½ inches long, then rip it to 2¾ inches wide.

4 From the 3½-inch wood stock, cut two side pieces 6¾ inches long with a 15° angle toward the front edge (about 5½ inches). Round over the front and bottom edges. Drill a pilot hole ⅜ inch (1 cm) in from the edge 1 inch (2.5 cm) down from the angle on the front edge, and another one centered along the bottom.

5 Use screws for all assembly. First, attach the side pieces to the back piece, using two screws per side, keeping the top of the sides flush with the angled top of the back.

6 Mount the door to the sides with two screws, again keeping the beveled door flush with the angled sides. Insert the floor flush with the bottom of the sides and screw into position.

7 Position the roof so the beveled edge is flush with the back and it overlaps both sides equally. Secure with two screws into each side.

8 Round over the exposed edges of the back. Drill two mounting holes in the back, if desired.

9 To finish, first sand smooth all the surfaces, then paint the roof forest green, allow to dry thoroughly, and paint the rest of the cottage sky blue.

DESIGNER: **Robin Clark**

GARDENER'S TIP

It is common in some areas to find ladybugs colonizing in the corners of ceilings in winter. If you have these little guests in your house, put them in a cotton or cheesecloth bag (not mesh, because their legs will get caught) with some peat or other organic matter for them to feed on. Store them for up to three months in the refrigerator. When you release them in the spring, spray them with sugar water, which will keep them grounded temporarily and encourage them to stay.

STAR MOSAIC BIRDHOUSE

I*f you don't have the time or the interest in making a birdhouse from scratch, try embellishing a purchased house with a colorful mosaic design. With a little creativity and planning, a plain birdhouse becomes a magnificent work of garden art that the neighborhood birds will enjoy.*

Materials and Tools

Preassembled birdhouse

Yellow spray paint, gloss

Assorted ceramic tiles

Ceramic tile adhesive

Ceramic tile grout (one tube)

Small pine cone

Pencil

Cloth rags

Protective eyeglasses

Tile nippers and/or a hammer

Small disposable palette knife
   or picnic knife

Latex gloves

Hot-glue gun

DESIGNER: **Tamara Miller**

GARDENER'S TIP *The best way to attract butterflies is to grow nectar plants that they are known to like, such as butterfly bush, butterfly weed, aster, and black-eyed Susans. A butterfly garden should be in a sunny spot that is protected from wind.*

Instructions

1 Though a hexagonal birdhouse works nicely with the star mosaic we have chosen here, feel free to use a house in any shape you like—and vary the design accordingly. Birdhouses in nontraditional shapes create a more interesting finished product. Remove perch from birdhouse (if applicable).

2 Spray-paint the outside of the birdhouse. We've used yellow to highlight the green and white mosaic design, but use whatever color best suits your design. Paint the inside of the opening with the same color paint.

3 Once the birdhouse has been painted, determine what your design will be. Sketch the design onto the front of the birdhouse with a pencil. Feel free to erase as needed until you are pleased with the design.

4 Wrap a ceramic tile in cloth rags. Wearing protective eyeglasses, strike the tile (through the cloth) with a hammer to break it into pieces. Use tile nippers to cut pieces into smaller shapes. Repeat this process with other ceramic tiles.

5 Arrange the tile pieces on the birdhouse in the shape of the design. (This is to make sure you have enough tiles to cover the entire design.) Use a hammer and/or tile nippers to cut additional pieces of tile as necessary.

6 Remove tiles from birdhouse, then apply a thin layer of tile adhesive to the front of the house with a small disposable palette knife or picnic knife. Working from the center of the design outward, place pieces of tile in the design area. (Be careful not to leave sharp edges around the opening where the birds will enter.) Allow adhesive to dry for at least 24 hours.

7 Apply tile grout according to manufacturer's instructions. (Wear latex gloves to protect your hands.) Allow grout to set for 24 hours. (You can find premixed grout at most home improvement stores; for this project, one tube should be sufficient.)

8 Hot-glue a pine cone in place underneath the opening for a perch.

the
Well-Decorated
GARDEN
Chapter 4

*Outdoor
Furnishings*

RUSTIC LOVESEAT

P art of the fun in creating rustic furniture is that your design will always be original, since it depends greatly on the materials you find in the woods. In fact, there's no limit to what you can make with vine and a little imagination. This "loveseat" can serve as a convenient resting spot for your visitors (be sure to use sturdy wood), or a charming plant stand evocative of a primeval forest.

Materials and Tools

Sapling wood (hickory, oak, ash, laurel), 2 to 3 inches (5 to 7.5 cm) in diameter (for the legs and braces)

1 x 12 inch board for the seat (actual dimensions are ¾ x 11¼ inches)

Pieces of green smoke vine (used here) or any other flexible vine, such as grapevine, laurel, or bittersweet, cut to varying lengths (for the back, arms, and trim)

Sheet moss

Saw

Hammer

Nails

DESIGNER: **Edith Howard**
FOR APPLEWOOD CRAFTS
(ASHEVILLE, NORTH CAROLINA)

Instructions

1 Determine how high you want the legs of your seat to be, then cut four pieces of sapling wood to that height. (The legs on the loveseat in the photograph are 15 inches [38 cm] high.) Make sure all four legs are exactly the same height.

2 Determine how wide you want the seat to be and cut the 1 x 12 board to that measurement. (The seat in the photograph is 24 inches [61 cm] long.) You can use more than one 1 x 12 board to make a wider seat, if desired.

3 Nail the sapling legs to the 1 x 12 board. To give the loveseat extra stability, attach additional sapling wood between the legs to create center braces. See diagram.

4 To add decorative trim, nail pieces of vine to the front and sides of the seat in a crisscross pattern as shown in the diagram and photograph. *Note*: For clarity, the diagram only shows a crisscross pattern on the side.

5 Nail pieces of vine to the sides of the seat to serve as armrests. You will want to twist, shape, and experiment with the vine pieces before nailing them in place. (The appearance of the armrests will depend on the size and shape of the available vine pieces.)

6 Do the same (see step 5) with larger pieces of vine to make the back of the seat. As you nail pieces in place, twist and interlock the vine pieces as shown in the photograph and the diagram.

7 Lay sheet moss on top of the seat. Attach narrow pieces of vine to the front and top of the seat with nails. The vine will help secure the moss to the seat.

GARDENER'S TIP *An interesting trellis can be "woven" quickly from long, thin branches or saplings. (See the trellis in the background [left] in the photograph on page 67.) Simply cut five or six straight pieces to the desired width, and five or six pieces to the desired height, then weave the pieces together as you would a basket. Make two of the vertical pieces extend slightly longer at the bottom to create a stand. Drive these pieces into the ground until the trellis is stable. You can make this sort of trellis any size—from any kind of wood.*

LOCUST-LOG ARBOR

DESIGNER: **Joel Cole**

A splendid garden arbor covered with a variety of climbing plants is a luxurious addition to any garden space—and a wonderful way to set apart an entryway or seating area. Though you can construct this arbor out of any variety of wood, locust is an excellent choice, because it is strong and decay-resistant.

Materials and Tools

4 large locust logs
(for corner posts)

12 medium locust logs
(for framing and top)

12 small locust limbs
(for sides)

Chain saw

Post-hole digger

Electric drill

Large metal screws

Large nails or wire

Instructions

1 First, you will need to decide what size you want the arbor to be. Determine both the height and the width—approximate measurements should be sufficient in most cases. *Note*: there is no need to worry about being exact when constructing this arbor, since it is a rustic structure.

2 Cut the four large locust logs to the desired height (see step 1). Make sure these four logs are approximately the same thickness and cut to approximately the same height.

3 Mark on the ground the location of the four large posts (using the predetermined width of the arbor [see step 1] as a guide), then dig four 2-foot (.6-m) holes with a post-hole digger. Place a large post in each of the four holes and tamp dirt around posts to secure in place.

4 Cut the 12 medium-sized logs: six logs to fit across the sides of the arbor (three on each side), and six logs to fit across the top (see diagram).

5 Use large metal screws to secure two of the medium-sized logs to the large corner posts on the inside top of the arbor as shown. (Use an electric drill to make a pilot hole first.) Nail or wire the four remaining side framing pieces to the inner sides of the arbor (two on each side) as shown.

6 Place the remaining six medium-sized pieces on top of the arbor as shown in the diagram and secure with nails or wire.

7 Cut the 12 small locust limbs to fit in a crisscross pattern as shown. Weave together these side pieces and wire to the frame.

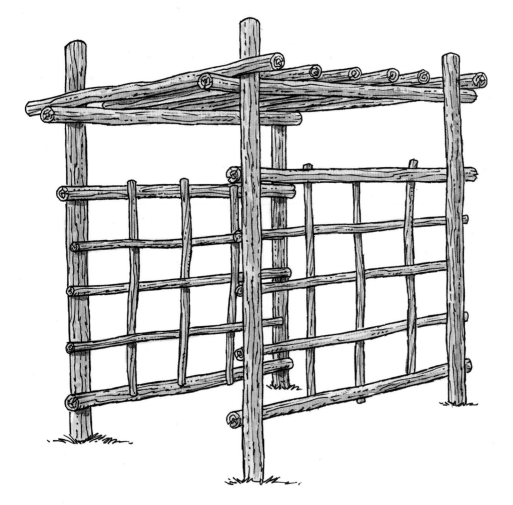

ARTIST'S GALLERY *Tinka Jordy*

Tinka Jordy has been a professional artist for 24 years. Though she is recognized primarily for her larger sculptural works in private, corporate, and public installations, salt-fired garden sculptures are a whimsical addition to her body of work.

RAKU FISH
Salt-fired stoneware and steel   PHOTO: Tinka Jordy

FLYING FROG
Salt-fired stoneware and steel   PHOTO: Tinka Jordy

BACKLESS GARDEN BENCH

hough the designer has used western red cedar for this bench, any high-quality exterior wood may be used without finishing. Pine or other woods can be used if the bench is to be painted.

Materials and Tools

⁵⁄₄-inch western red cedar (actual thickness is 1 inch):
  two pieces 8 feet x 7¼ inches (for seat slats and stringers),
  one piece 3 feet x 5½ inches (for straight sides of legs),
  and one piece 3 feet x 7¼ inches (for angled sides of legs)

Forty 1⁵⁄₈-inch (4.1-cm) coarse-thread deck screws (or equivalent)

Eight 2-inch (5-cm) coarse-thread deck screws (or equivalent)

Wood water seal (optional)

Saw

Electric drill with ⅛-inch (.3-cm) bit

Screwdriver

Router with ¼-inch (.5-cm) round-over bit (optional)

Fine sandpaper

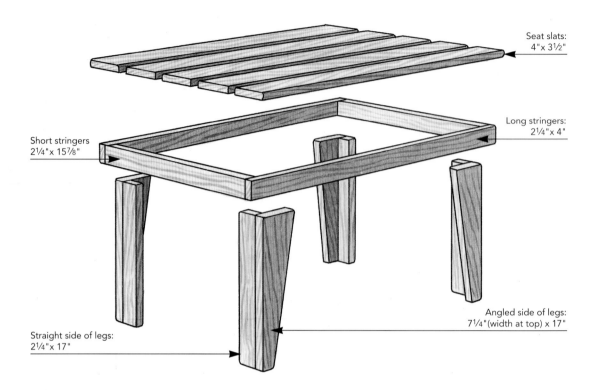

Seat slats:
4" x 3½"

Long stringers:
2¼" x 4"

Short stringers
2¼" x 15⅞"

Angled side of legs:
7¼" (width at top) x 17"

Straight side of legs:
2¼" x 17"

Instructions

1 Cut the two 8-foot boards in half to create four 4-foot boards. From these boards, rip five seat slats 3¼ inches wide and two long stringers 2¼ inches wide. (You will use two and a half 4-foot boards for seat slats and one board for the stringers.) Cut two short stringers 2¼ x 15⅞ inches from the remaining pieces.

2 Cut the two 3-foot boards into 17-inch lengths to create two 5¼- x 17-inch pieces and two 7¼- x 17-inch pieces. From the narrow (5¼-inch) boards, rip four leg pieces 2¼ inches wide. Measure and mark a point 2 inches in from diagonally opposite corners of the wide (7¼-inch) pieces. Draw a line connecting these points, then cut along the line to create four angled legs.

3 Drill two pilot holes ½ inch (1.5 cm) in from the short ends of all five seat slats as well as the long stringers.

4 Attach the short stringers to the long stringers at the ends using eight 2-inch (5-cm) screws, keeping all edges flush. For the rest of the bench assembly, you will use the 1⅝-inch (4.1-cm) screws.

5 Drill pilot holes ½ inch (1.5 cm) in and 3 inches (7.5 cm) up along the straight edge of the angled legs. Screw the straight leg pieces to the angled leg pieces.

6 Round over all edges with a router or sandpaper.

7 Place a leg in each corner of the stringer assembly with the angled portion of the leg pieces along the long sides of the bench. With the top of the leg flush to the top of the stringer, secure leg with two screws in each wide leg and one screw in each narrow portion.

8 Lay the outermost seat slats on the top of the leg assembly with a ⅛-inch (.3-cm) overhang on the long edge and flush with the short ends. Secure with screws at each end. Equally space the three remaining slats, then screw them into position as well.

9 Sand all exposed surfaces. No finish is necessary, though we sprayed this bench with a water seal for added protection.

PATIO CHAIR CUSHIONS

DESIGNER: **Carol Parks**

$\mathbb{T}$his cushion design features an attached strap that buttons around the back legs of the chair to hold the cushion in place; this strap doubles as a carrying handle. We used Sunbrella fabric, which was developed fairly recently for outdoor use. It is water repellent, mildew resistant, and resists sun fading. The fabric is not plastic coated, so it is comfortable to sit on—unlike the plastic-coated outdoor fabrics, which tend to be sticky (and hard to sew).

Materials and Tools

(For each cushion)

Foam, 1 to 2 inches (2.5 to 5 cm) thick. (Use high-density foam designed for seating so the cushion won't "bottom out" when you sit on it. Upholstery suppliers stock this and will cut to size.)

Fabric, according to measurements of the chair (see below)

Piping cord

2 large buttons

Heavy-duty zipper. Upholstery materials shops sell this by the inch, cut to your measurements. The zipper should be the length of the cushion back measurement plus approximately 6 inches (15 cm).

Metal carpenter's square and sharp craft knife (optional)

Sewing machine

Instructions

1 To make a pattern, measure the width and length of the chair seat. If the cushion is to be shaped around chair legs (as ours are), it is a good idea to make a paper pattern. Fold the pattern in half lengthwise—front to back—to make sure both sides are the same.

2 Using the measurements of your chair or the pattern, cut the foam (or have it cut). If you do the cutting, use a heavy metal carpenter's square and a very sharp craft knife to make the cuts straight down.

3 Use the pattern to cut a cushion top and bottom, adding seam allowance around all edges. Don't add ease—the cover should fit tightly. Mark center back and corners on the seamline.

4 To make the boxing strip (the sides) and zipper gusset, measure the circumference of the pattern. The zipper will be installed close to the lower edge of the cushion so that the strap can be sewn to the upper, or overlapping, section of the zipper gusset. Cut an upper and lower zipper gusset piece: in length, the length of the zipper (which includes seam allowance); in width, cut each approximately 2½ times the cushion thickness. The width isn't critical at this point; it will be adjusted after the zipper is installed.

5 To make the remaining portion of the boxing strip, subtract the *finished* zipper gusset length from the total circumference measurement. Cut a strip this length, adding seam allowance at each end. In width, cut it to the cushion thickness with seam allowance added at both edges.

6 To make the piping, double the circumference measurement and add approximately 6 inches (15 cm). Cut a bias strip to this length; in width, cut the strip to the diameter of the cord plus two seam allowances.

7 To determine the strap length, position the foam on the chair and measure from the desired point in front of one leg, around the leg, across the back, and around the other leg. Allow a little ease, and add approximately 6 inches (15 cm) total for the button loops. Plan for the width of the strap to be slightly less than the cushion thickness, or narrower, if you wish. Cut the strap four times this width measurement.

8 To make the piping, wrap the fabric evenly around the cord and stitch not quite as closely as possible to the cord, using a zipper or piping foot on your sewing machine.

9 Install the zipper. Fold one zipper gusset piece in half lengthwise, right side out, and press a crease. This will be the lower or underlying piece. Stitch to the right side of the zipper tape, aligning the crease with the stitching line on the tape. Fold and crease the other gusset piece in the same way. Position it on the zipper so that it overlaps the stitched edge of the lower section. Stitch to the zipper tape along the tape stitching line. Stitch across each end, at the seamline and again about ½ inch (1.5 cm) inside, taking care not to hit the zipper teeth.

10 Match the width of the zipper gusset to the remaining boxing strip section. Plan that the fold of the zipper overlap will be approximately ¼ inch (.5 cm) above the seamline that joins the strip to the cushion bottom. Trim the strip accordingly.

11 Stitch the upper end of the zipper section to the remaining boxing strip section. Leave the other ends of the pieces unsewn for now in case the fit needs to be fine-tuned when the cover is assembled. Mark the center of the finished zipper strip on both seamlines.

12 Stitch piping to the cushion top and bottom sections. Mark a beginning point at some inconspicuous place on the piece. Leave about 1 inch

15 To make the strap, fold the strip in half lengthwise, right side out; press. Fold the raw edges in to the center crease and press again. Stitch close to both long edges (the ends remain unfinished for now). Mark the center.

16 Fit the upper cover section over the foam and place it on the chair. Fit the strap in place, matching center backs. Mark button positions in front of each back leg of the chair. Fold under each end of the strap to form a loop that will fit over the button, and pin. Trim the ends if necessary. Mark, on the strap and on the boxing strip of the cushion, a point inside each back leg at which the strap will be sewn to the overlapping part of the zipper gusset.

17 Stitch each end of the strap to the strap itself to make the button loops, using a zigzag stitch to overcast the raw ends at the same time. Then stitch an X for security. Stitch the strap to the cushion cover at the marked points, stitching an X at a point between the piping seam and the zipper stitching. Pin the strap ends to the center of the cushion top to keep them out of the way while you finish the construction.

18 Open the zipper. Stitch the cover bottom in place as you did the top. Sew the buttons at the marked points, placing a folded fabric scrap behind each for support. Make a long thread shank to accommodate the thickness of the button loop.

(2.5 cm) of piping extending beyond this point and begin stitching at the marked point, right sides together, raw edges of the piping aligned with the edge of the cover. Around outer corners, clip the piping seam allowance at close intervals to fit the curves. If there are inner corners, as at the back legs of the chair shown, clip notches from the piping seam allowance for fit.

13 At the end, stop stitching approximately 2 inches (5 cm) short of the starting point. Cut off the piping about 1 inch (2.5 cm) past the starting point. Unsew the piping seam along this length and clip away 1 inch (2.5 cm) of the cord. On the end, turn the fabric edge to the inside so the fold is ½ inch (1.5 cm) beyond the trimmed cord end. At the beginning, trim the

unstitched piping to ½ inch (1.5 cm) beyond the starting point. Trim away all of the seam allowance on this extension. Now slip the finished end of the piping over this end and finish stitching to the cushion section. Whipstitch around the join by hand if desired. Attach piping to the other cushion section in the same way.

14 Stitch the boxing strip to the upper cushion section, right sides together, beginning approximately 3 inches (7.5 cm) from the lower end of the zipper strip and matching center backs. Stitch just inside the piping stitching line. At the end, check the fit and fold under the seam allowance to overlap the zipper gusset seam allowance, then complete the stitching.

TILE SIDE TABLE

ere, *a designer has taken an inexpensive table found at a yard sale and transformed it into a gorgeous garden side table. Thrift stores and flea markets are also great places to find tables for this purpose; look for ones that will withstand the elements. This project is a superb way to use ceramic tile left over from other projects.*

Materials and Tools

Square or rectangular side table (see above)

Ceramic tile in assorted colors and shapes

Ceramic tile adhesive

Ceramic tile grout

Protective sealant (optional)

Plastic (to cover work surface)

Tile cutter (optional)

Small disposable palette knife or disposable picnic knife

Protective eyeglasses (optional)

Latex gloves

Barely damp sponge or lint-free rags

DESIGNER: **Tamara Miller**

Instructions

1 Clean the surface of the table thoroughly and position table on a piece of plastic on a flat work surface.

2 Arrange assorted ceramic tiles on the tabletop until you are pleased with the design. Depending on the shape and size of your chosen table, you may need to use a tile cutter to size tile pieces to fit around the edges of the table.

3 When the design is final, remove the tiles and position on a nearby flat surface in the exact arrangement you've chosen for the tabletop.

4 Spread a layer of ceramic tile adhesive on the tabletop (refer to the manufacturer's instructions) with a small disposable palette knife or picnic knife, then position tiles on the tabletop, one at a time, in the chosen configuration. Allow adhesive to dry for at least 24 hours.

5 Apply grout to tabletop according to manufacturer's instructions. (Wear latex gloves to protect your hands.) Work the grout into the spaces between the tiles. Cover the entire stone in this manner. After about 15 minutes (or the amount of time specified by the manufacturer's instructions), remove excess grout and grout haze with a barely damp sponge or lint-free rags.

6 Allow the grout to dry according to the manufacturer's instructions. You may give your table additional protection by coating it with a protective sealant that is compatible with the grout.

ARTIST'S GALLERY

Ivy Fletcher & Pat Riesenburger

Ivy Fletcher and Pat Riesenburger teamed up to pursue their passions for art and gardening in 1994. Today, the pair focuses on creating mosaic art for the garden. According to Ivy, "The intent of our work is to embellish nature with forms, textures, and colors that evoke joy."

LEFT: GAZING GLOBE, 1998
Glass, rock, broken dish mosaic on cement
PHOTO: Beckett Lake Nursery, Florida

BELOW LEFT: GAZING GLOBE, 1998
Glass and rock mosaic on concrete
PHOTO: Beckett Lake Nursery, Florida

BELOW RIGHT: GAZING GLOBE, 1998
Glass and rock mosaic on concrete
PHOTO: Beckett Lake Nursery, Florida

STENCILED TULIP PRIVACY FENCE

DESIGNER: **Kathleen Burke**

An inexpensive section of fencing (available at home centers) may be all you need to give a problem area of your garden some much-needed privacy—and added color to boot. Of course, this design can be varied to your liking and to match the colors of your garden. For extra decorative effect, attach sturdy hooks to the fence and hang terra-cotta pots filled with bright flowers or climbing plants.

Materials and Tools

Section of prefabricated wooden fencing

Exterior wood primer, white

Exterior latex paint: white, pale yellow, red, and green

Tulip stencil (see below) or other stencil of your choice

Piece of cardboard or any other stencil material

Assorted paintbrushes

Masking tape (optional)

Craft knife

Spray shellac (optional)

Chunks of upholstery foam or other stenciling applicator

Newsprint or a rag (optional)

Instructions

1 Apply two coats of primer to the fencing and allow to dry thoroughly. *Note*: It is important that the fencing be completely dry before you begin painting. This is of particular consideration if you are painting a section of fence that is already installed outside. If you are painting outside, make sure there has been at least two days of dry weather before you paint.

2 Paint the entire fence section white with exterior latex paint; you may need two coats for complete coverage. Allow paint to dry thoroughly.

3 When white paint is completely dry, paint every other board pale yellow. Allow yellow paint to dry thoroughly. (If you do not have a steady hand, you may want to use masking tape to cover the edges of the adjacent white boards. Another option is to touch up any messy spots with white paint later.)

4 You can either use the tulip stencil we've provided or use any other stencil of your choosing. Scale up the stencil to the appropriate size for your fence. (Any print shop will be able to help you with this.) Trace the stencil on a thin, stiff piece of cardboard or any other stencil material and cut it out with a sharp craft knife. If you use cardboard and plan to reuse the stencil, you can seal the cardboard with shellac on both sides to prevent the paint from bleeding into the board.

5 Position the stencil on the fence where you want the first design to be, and tape down the edges to keep it from moving while you stencil. Apply red and green exterior latex paint to the tulip stencil design with small chunks of dense upholstery foam. (Upholstery foam creates a rough, grainy texture that is particularly appropriate for an outdoor decoration, but you can use any stenciling tool you prefer.) Make sure you do not have too much paint on the stenciling tool; dab it on newsprint or a rag to remove excess, if necessary.

6 After both colors (red and green) have been painted, carefully remove stencil. Check the back of the stencil to see if there has been any bleed-through before positioning it back on the fence for the next section of stenciling.

7 Repeat steps 5 and 6 as many times as necessary to cover the section of fence.

GARDENER'S TIP *If your garden is short on privacy, try affixing a trellis to the top of your garden wall for added height. Grow decorative climbing plants on the wall and trellis for a rich, natural barrier.*

GARDEN TABLE

A colorful wooden table, made with stock lumber and painted in hues reminiscent of bright summer flowers, is a welcome and versatile addition to any outdoor space. You can set it for a garden dinner party or convert into a handy (and quite handsome) potting bench. Mismatched wooded chairs, found at thrift stores, yard sales, and flea markets, can easily be painted to create a charming outdoor dining set.

GARDENER'S TIP

Position plants at different levels in your garden to create visual interest, either by creating raised beds, grouping an assortment of containers, or choosing plants that grow to different heights.

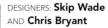

Materials and Tools

Lumber: We used a variety of leftover lumber, but if you plan to purchase new material, we recommend pressure-treated lumber. Wood measurements are given in standard, nominal sizes: for actual dimensions see chart on page 83.

Frame

    Long sides:
    two 2 x 4s cut 66 inches long

    Short sides:
    two 2 x 4s cut 30 inches long

    Center brace:
    one 2 x 4 cut 21½ inches long

Legs

    Four 4 x 4s cut 29 inches long

Apron

    Long sides:
    two 1 x 4s cut 67½ inches long

    Short sides:
    two 1 x 4s cut 30 inches long

Tabletop

    Three 1 x 12s cut 72 inches long

Latex paint in assorted colors

Spar varnish

2½-inch (6.5-cm) decking screws, 24

2-inch (5-cm) finishing nails (approximately 50)

Circular saw and chisel

Carpenter's square

Hatchet or plane (optional)

Sander or file

Paintbrush

Sandpaper

Wooden chairs (optional)

Instructions

1 To build the table frame, notch the 2 x 4s 3½ inches (9 cm) from the end at each outside corner as shown in Diagram 1. (The designers used a circular saw with the blade depth set at 3½ inches [9 cm], then chiseled out the notches.)

2 On a flat, level surface, snap the frame pieces into the notches (see Diagram 1) and place one decking screw in the center of each notch joint.

3 Attach the center brace with two decking screws on each side. It is a good idea to check the squareness of all corners with a carpenter's square before securing center brace.

4 Attach legs to frame at each outside corner. Use two decking screws where frame meets each side of leg.

5 Begin the tabletop by first setting the assembled table base right side up. Using 2-inch (5-cm) finishing nails, attach the three 1 x 12 tabletop planks, leaving an ⅛-inch (.3-cm) gap between each board for water runoff.

6 Attach apron on all four sides, beginning with the long sides. Drive two finishing nails into each leg and two finishing nails into each inside frame end.

7 If desired, round the outside corner of each leg with either a hatchet (for a rustic texture), or a plane (for a smooth texture). Round-off the tabletop and apron edges with a file or a sander.

8 Apply several layers of brightly colored paint to the table, allowing each color to dry thoroughly between coats, then lightly sanding between each color application. (These designers used mismatched colors from a markdown table at a local home center.)

9 Continue to reapply coats of paint and to sand until desired effect is achieved (see photographs). To create matching chairs, use the same painting technique on wooden chairs.

10 Apply several (two or more) coats of spar varnish to the table. Make sure you apply varnish to the underside of the table and between the tabletop boards. Also, pay attention to nail locations—they must be well covered with varnish. If you have painted chairs to match, they also need several coats of spar varnish. *Note*: If using chairs with solid bottoms, drill holes (for water runoff) in the seats if the chairs will be left out in the rain.

Legs: 3½" x 3½"
(common 4 x 4)

Frame length,
short sides: 30"

Apron length,
short sides: 30"

Tabletop
width: 34"

Apron length,
long sides: 67½"

Center brace
length: 21½"

Frame length,
long sides: 66"

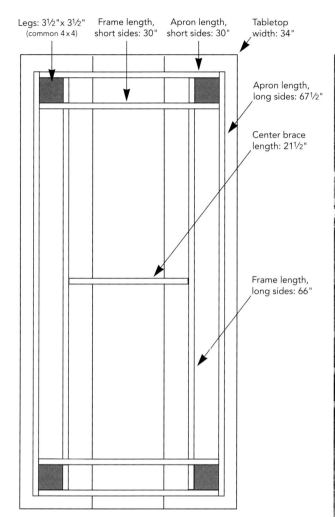

DIAGRAM 1. Table viewed from underneath

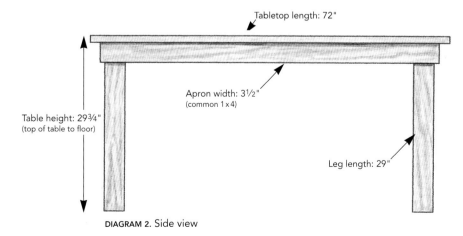

Actual Dimensions
for Stock Lumber

$2 \times 4 = 1\frac{1}{2}" \times 3\frac{1}{2}"$

$4 \times 4 = 3\frac{1}{2}" \times 3\frac{1}{2}"$

$1 \times 4 = \frac{3}{4}" \times 3\frac{1}{2}"$

$1 \times 12 = \frac{3}{4}" \times 11\frac{1}{4}"$

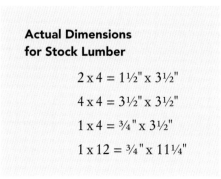

Tabletop length: 72"

Apron width: 3½"
(common 1 x 4)

Table height: 29¾"
(top of table to floor)

Leg length: 29"

DIAGRAM 2. Side view

the
Well-Decorated
GARDEN

Chapter 5

Wind
Water &
Light

GARDEN TORCHES

hese garden lights will cast an enchanting, fiery radiance on any garden setting. They are especially handsome—and useful, since they provide light and possibly scent—when positioned at an entryway or near outdoor seating.

Materials and Tools

(for one torch)

Black aluminum screening, approx. 13 x 17 inches (33 x 43 cm)

½-inch (1.5-cm) diameter copper piping, 5 feet (1.5 m)

18-gauge copper wire, 4 to 6 feet (1.2 to 1.8 m)

½-inch (1.5-cm) male adapter

½-inch (1.5-cm) floor flange

Small container candle (see page 86)

⅝-inch (1.6-cm) hose clamp

Scissors or wire cutters

Stapler (optional)

Hot-glue gun (optional)

Instructions

1 Wrap aluminum screen into a cone shape with an opening at the narrow end large enough to fit over the end of the copper pipe.

2 Place screen cone over the end of the copper pipe so that about 6 inches (15 cm) of the pipe is inside the cone. Tighten a hose clamp around the bottom of the cone so that it will remain secure on the pipe.

3 Wrap copper wire tightly and evenly above clamp up to 3 to 4 inches (7.5 to 10 cm) from the top of the pipe. Make sure the cone is open enough to accommodate the floor flange (see step 6 below). Cut wire with scissors or wire cutters and secure end under wrapped wire. Remove hose clamp.

4 Crimp top edges of screen by folding over by hand and pressing in place.

5 Secure the overlapping ends of the screen by either threading the screen with a piece of copper wire or securing with a stapler.

6 Place a male adapter on the end of the copper pipe (inside the screen cone); then connect floor flange to the male adapter. (Male adapters and floor flanges are available at home supply stores.) The floor flange will create a flat surface on which the candle will sit. See detail photograph (left) for a close-up view of torch construction.

7 Once torch is securely positioned in the ground (and level) place container candle (see page 86) on floor flange. You can place a small amount of hot glue on the bottom of the candle, if desired, to help hold the candle in place.

DESIGNER: **Pamela Brown**

DESIGNER: **Pamela Brown**

Glass containers help protect outdoor candles from breezes. Container candles make great garden accessories; use them with the garden torches (see page 84), line them up along a moss-covered wall, or scent them with citronella and light them to repel insects.

Materials and Tools (for one jar)

4- to 8-ounce (113- to 226-g) glass jar

Paraffin wax, approximately ½ pound or 228 g (amount will vary, depending on the size of the jar)

4 inches (10 cm) wire-core wick. (Ask candle supply store for the size that corresponds with specific jar diameter.)

Citronella oil or any other scented oil of your choice (optional)

Double-boiler setup

Knife

Candy thermometer

Metal cup with a handle, or a dipper

Piece of wire, a long nail, or a pencil

CONTAINER CANDLES

Instructions

1 Make sure the jar will hold hot wax by filling it with near-boiling water. If the jar holds up, it will make a great candle container.

2 Heat water over medium heat in the bottom of a double-boiler setup. Chop wax into pieces with a knife. Place wax pieces in the top of the double-boiler setup. Clip candy thermometer to the side of the pan and heat wax until it reaches 155° to 165° F (68° to 74° C). Do not leave the pot unattended for any reason while the hot wax is melting! It is very important that the wax not get too hot. The flash point (point at which the wax will ignite) varies for different types of wax; make sure you know what it is for your wax before you begin.

3 When the wax is completely melted and has reached the correct temperature (see step 2), prime the wick by dipping it into the wax. Set wick aside to cool.

4 If you wish, add citronella oil (or any other scented oil) to the wax at this point.

5 Turn off heat. Using a cup with a handle or a dipper, scoop wax into the jar until jar is filled.

6 Let wax cool a few minutes, then stand wick into the center of the candle. Tie the end of the wick to a piece of wire, a nail, or a pencil and place wire or pencil across top of jar to keep wick centered.

7 As the candle cools, a well will form in the center of the candle. Check the candle every few minutes. When well forms, pierce the wax around the wick with a nail or a piece of wire, then pour more melted wax into the jar to top it off.

8 Allow candle to harden completely, then trim wick to ¼ inch (.5 cm).

A GARDEN takes on a magical feel at night. Though a full moon is the best night lighting, artificial lighting is the most practical way to make your outdoor space accessible and enjoyable when the sun goes down. Adding light to your garden need not be an intimidating undertaking—and it does not necessarily require any previous knowledge of electrical wiring.

First, determine what you want and need to light. If you have a treasured Japanese maple, then you may want to position a spotlight underneath the tree so that the filigreed leaves cast an interesting

shadow on the ground. Certain areas of your garden may be more accessible at night—those closest to your house, for example—and you may want to start there.

Certain architectural aspects of your garden (gazebos, arbors, benches, or arches) may need some lighting to be functional after dark. A treasured sundial (though useless as a timepiece when the sun goes down) may be just as attractive when illuminated at night.

Determine whether the items you want to highlight should be lit from above with a spotlight (called *uplighting*) or below with suspended lights (called *downlighting*). If you have a path or walkway (see page 112), consider path lighting. Be careful not to add too much lighting, though; the contrast between light and darkness is what makes the evening garden interesting and magical. (You should strive for a subtle, delicately lit effect, not the football-stadium look.)

Do some research into what lighting is available and affordable. You may want to obscure the source of light or prominently display decorative fixtures. In the case of the latter, choose fixtures that fit into your overall garden design. Experiment with different lighting configurations, and don't hesitate to change and move as needed to create the desired effect.

If you decide to install electrically powered lighting, you have two choices. You can hire a licensed electrician to install your fixture; professionally installed lighting tends to be more expensive and higher voltage. It is possible to purchase low voltage lighting kits that you install yourself. This process, in most cases, is relatively easy, but the quality of the fixtures tends to be lower.

Water and lighting go hand in hand. When light catches water, it can create a wonderful effect. Swimming pools are obvious choices for accent lighting, as the clear, blue water lends itself so nicely to underwater lighting. This technique does not always work with the murky water often found in ponds and lakes; you may want to project light onto these bodies of water from above. A professional electrician should be consulted to insure safe installation of any underwater lighting.

Nonelectrical lighting is a quick and easy alternative to electrical lighting. Luminaries are a wonderful addition to any garden; they are easy to make and very safe. A variety of stake votive holders and lanterns are now available, each casting a unique glow. Use your imagination and experiment with different forms of lighting to create the perfect evening garden setting.

COPPER FLOWER
CANDLE STANDS

uests will ooh and aah over delightful copper flowers—and certainly never guess they're made from toilet tank floats! These candle holders make great pathway lighting. Place a votive candle inside the bloom and they will cast a warm, wonderful glow on an evening garden party.

DESIGNER:
Janice Rieves

88

Materials and Tools
(for one holder)

Copper toilet tank float

Liquid silicone

Steel or brass rod (with a diameter that is slightly smaller than hole in the float base)

Putty epoxy

Enamel copper paint

Sheet of thin copper (optional)

Spray lacquer or polyurethane (optional)

Votive candle

Steel wool

Electric drill with ½-inch (1.5-cm) bit

Scissors or tin snips

Gloves (optional)

Pencil (optional)

Needle-nose pliers

Paintbrush

GARDENER'S TIP *To best highlight your garden at night, position garden lighting near your favorite flowers or garden decorations.*

Instructions

1 Clean the outside of the copper float with steel wool.

2 Drill a ½-inch (1.5-cm) hole in the center of the top of the copper float. Using a pair of scissors or tin snips, cut out a small circle around the drilled hole. (The bottom of the float will already have a hole where stem will be attached.)

3 To make a flower petal, use scissors or tin snips to make a straight cut down along the rib to the middle of the float. Count over two ridges and cut down again to the same point. Repeat this procedure all the way around the float, bending the previously cut petal backwards and down each time to prevent getting cut on the copper edges. (The cut edges and tips of the petals are extremely sharp; you may want to use gloves.)

4 To make curly stamens (see photograph, left), cut every other petal in half lengthwise and wrap the narrow copper piece around a pencil.

5 To create veining in the petals, use needle-nose pliers to crimp a v-shape in the petals. (Both candle holders shown in the photograph have crimped petals.)

6 To create double blossoms (see photograph, left), cut two copper flowers, one with curly stamens, and the other without (see steps 3 and 4). Cut a circle out of the base of the flower that has stamens—this flower will go inside the other flower. Squeeze a line of silicone around the inside of the flower without stamens and press the other copper flower inside to secure.

7 Use a straight steel or brass rod to make the flower stem. Knead a marble-size piece of putty epoxy for two to three minutes. (Do not overwork epoxy, as it hardens quickly.) Push the end of the brass fitting into the hole in the bottom of the tank float. Press the epoxy around the fitting, making sure there is good contact. Use additional epoxy as needed to secure stem to flower. After the epoxy dries, cover entire stem with copper paint.

8 If desired, cut a leaf out of thin copper sheeting, then cut a notch in the copper leaf on both sides, just up from the base of the leaf. Wrap the notched area around the stem and pack with putty epoxy to secure. Allow to dry thoroughly, then dab with copper paint to conceal epoxy.

9 If you do not want your flower to become green with age (verdigris), spray the entire surface with spray lacquer or polyurethane.

10 Position stem in ground so that copper flower stands straight. Place votive candle inside flower.

BEACH GLASS WIND CHIMES

Beach glass is any glass debris—anything from shards of beer bottles to ruins from shipwrecks—that has been tumbled in the sea, worn smooth, and become somewhat cloudy in appearance. It can be found along most beaches, particularly in New England, and is a wonderful material for a variety of craft projects. Here, we've combined it with an interesting piece of driftwood to create a set of lovely wind chimes.

DESIGNER: **Julie Anne Eason**

Materials and Tools

Assorted beach glass, approximately 15 pieces

Multipronged jewelry end caps, approximately 15

Small jump rings, approximately 15

Piece of driftwood

7 small eye screws

60 inches (150 cm) fishing line

12-inch (30.5-cm) chain

White craft glue

Needle-nose pliers

Instructions

1 Select the pieces of beach glass you would like to use, and clean and dry each piece thoroughly. Shape an end cap to the corner of each piece of beach glass and secure the end cap to glass with craft glue. Use needle-nose pliers to attach one jump ring to each end cap.

2 Screw five eye screws along the bottom of a piece of driftwood and two eye screws to the top of the driftwood at each edge. (Be sure to choose a piece of driftwood that is appropriate for the size of the beach glass.)

3 Cut the fishing line into five 12-inch (30.5-cm) pieces, then tie two or three pieces of glass to each piece of line as shown in the photograph. (Vary the number and arrangement of the beach glass as desired.)

4 Tie one string of glass to each eye screw on the bottom of the piece of driftwood.

5 Attach a 12-inch (30.5-cm) length of chain to the two eye screws on top of the driftwood to serve as a hanger.

Stefan Bonitz

Stefan Bonitz creates functional art, lighting, and furniture in a variety of styles ranging from folk art to high design. Working almost solely with recycled found metal objects became the primary focus of Stefan's work when he started Steebo Design in July 1995.

TOP LEFT: FORGED FLOWERS
Found metal objects
PHOTO: Evan Bracken

LEFT: SPACEBOY AND DOG
Found and recovered steel
PHOTO: Evan Bracken

BOTTOM LEFT: TRELLIS
Found and recovered steel
PHOTO: Evan Bracken

BOTTOM CENTER: GONG BELL
Found and recovered steel
PHOTO: Evan Bracken

BOTTOM RIGHT: GARDEN ALIEN
Found metal objects
PHOTO: Evan Bracken

LAVA ROCK CASCADE FOUNTAIN

Nothing soothes and calms like the gentle cascade of water in the garden. Small fountain pumps are available at garden centers and are very inexpensive. Lava rocks work well in small fountains, because they aerate water, clean themselves, and will not accumulate slime and dirt like other rocks or pebbles.

GARDENER'S TIP *Any garden setting is enhanced by the sound of trickling water, even if the source is hidden. Incorporate moving water into your garden to create a peaceful ambience.*

Materials and Tools

Lava rocks in assorted sizes (available at garden supply stores)—you will need four to six large rocks

Small submersible fountain pump

Plastic terra-cotta planter dish, 16 inches (40.5 cm) in diameter

8 inches (20.5 cm) sturdy plastic tubing, ½ inch (1.5 cm) in diameter

Mint or any water-friendly plants of your choice

Ceramic frog or other decorative feature (optional)

Garden hose

Electric drill with ¾-inch (2-cm) bit

Craft knife

Instructions

1 Use a garden hose to thoroughly rinse lava rocks outside. Lava rocks create a lot of red dust, so make sure the rocks are very clean before you begin to construct the fountain.

2 Position the pump toward the back of the planter dish and attach tubing to the water outlet on the submersible pump. *Note:* You can use a terra-cotta planter dish (instead of plastic) if you seal it first with a protective polyurethane coating. Otherwise, the terra-cotta, a porous substance, will allow water to escape.

3 Cover pump and planter dish with a layer of small lava rocks. Position additional small- and medium-sized rocks in planter dish in a pleasing arrangement so that pump, planter dish bottom, and plastic tubing are concealed.

4 Experiment with stacking larger rocks and determine how you would like them to be arranged to create the cascade. Drill a ¾-inch (2-cm) hole through the larger rocks and fit the plastic tubing up through these drilled holes. When drilling, it is helpful to pour a small amount of water through the drilled space, to prevent the drill bit and the rock from getting too hot.

5 Pour water into the rock-filled planter dish. Position large rocks around the plastic tube. Plug pump into an electric outlet and check the water cascade.

6 Unplug pump, then make any necessary changes to the arrangement of the rocks in the fountain. Use a craft knife to cut the plastic tube flush with top rock, so that the tube is not visible.

7 Wash the roots of the mint plants clean of any dirt and insert plants into fountain. (Any other water-friendly plants will work—ask for suggestions at your favorite garden supply store.) Place ceramic frog or any other decorative feature on rocks in fountain, if desired.

8 To transport a fountain with a plastic base, use a siphon to remove the water, then slide fountain onto a sturdy board.

DESIGNER: **Pamella Wilson**

GARDENER'S SUNDIAL

This simple sundial features a stately cement gnomon embellished with gold leaf. Metal house numbers are used for the dial, but this can easily be varied to fit your garden style; numbers can also be etched in cement slabs or painted on handmade tiles. See page 97 for more information on sundials.

Materials and Tools

1 x 6 pine board (actual dimensions ¾ x 5½ inches), 4½ feet (1.4 m)

2 pieces of ½-inch (1.5-cm) plywood, each 15 x 24 inches

Plastic sun stencil

Cement mix

Gold leaf or gold paint

Oil furniture finish

Aluminum house numbers (available at home centers and hardware stores)

Threaded rod

Nuts to fit threaded rod, two per house number

Saw

Nails/screws

Craft glue

Motor oil

Rubber mallet

Clean rag

Hacksaw

Cyanoacrylate glue

Instructions

1 Rip the 1 x 6 pine board into boards with the following dimensions: one 2½ x 24 inches (board A), one 2½ x 20¾ inches (board B), and one 2½ x 9 inches (board C). Cut 45° angle cuts in one side of boards B and C (see diagram).

2 Use nails or screws to assemble the pine boards and one piece of the plywood as shown in the illustration. This will be the mold for the gnomon.

3 Tack the plastic sun stencil on the side of the mold (see photograph for placement) with craft glue. (Plastic stencils in a variety of shapes are available at craft supply stores.)

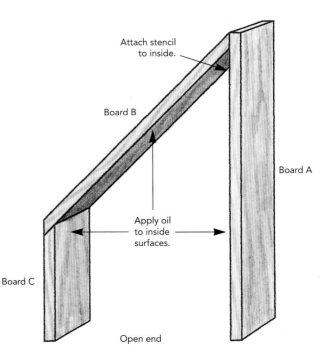

Attach stencil to inside.

Board B

Board A

Apply oil to inside surfaces.

Board C

Open end

GARDENER'S TIP *A planting of night-blooming flowers and a few well-placed lights will help make your garden an enjoyable outdoor living space— even after the sun goes down.*

DESIGNER: **Olivier Rollin**

4 Brush motor oil on the inner surfaces of the wooden mold and on one side of the second piece of plywood. Finish the mold by securing the second plywood piece to the wooden assembly with nails or screws.

5 Position the mold upright with the open end up. Place mold in a secure spot where it will not tip over easily. The easiest method of preparing the mold for the concrete is to dig a hole in the ground, deep enough to hold approximately a third of the mold, then tamp the dirt down around the mold to secure.

6 Mix the cement according to the manufacturer's instructions. Pour the cement into the mold, taking care not to entrap air bubbles. Tap the sides of the mold with a rubber mallet to release air pockets.

7 Allow cement to cure/dry according to manufacturer's instructions, then carefully disassemble the mold and remove the concrete piece. Remove the stencil; a sun indentation will remain on the gnomon.

8 Apply gold leaf to the inside of the sun indentation according to the manufacturer's instructions, or paint the inside of the indentation with gold paint. (Gold leaf is widely available at craft supply stores.) Apply oil finish to the gnomon with a clean rag.

9 If you want your sundial numbers to be elevated (ours are, as shown in the photograph), you will need to attach threaded rods and nuts to the

metal house numbers. The rods will be pushed into the ground to secure the numbers in place. You will need to buy long rods of threaded metal, then cut the metal into lengths, according to what you need. (Experiment with different lengths where you plan to install the sundial.) Cut the rods with a hacksaw, then attach a nut to the house number and a nut to the rod. Connect the rod to the house number.

10 Install the cement gnomon either in a flat area in your garden or in a shallow pond. Though installing

the sundial in a level section of lawn is easy and attractive, be aware that this method of installation makes the numbers quite difficult to trim around. You can use a base of gravel, moss, or low-growing plants as an alternative. The gnomon will need to be placed approximately 4 inches (10 cm) into the ground for stability. Stones or gravel can be used to help stabilize the heavy cement gnomon in a pond. (The numbers should be just at or above water level for the best effect.) For extra hold, embed the threaded rods into a concrete pad before installing the numbers underwater.

Sundials

Long valued as timepieces as well as works of art, sundials are ancient devices that measure the passage of time according to the rising and setting of the sun. The earliest existing sundial, one found buried in Egypt, is now held in the Berlin Museum. It bears the name Thutmose III, who ruled from 1504 to 1450 BC.

The sundial was common from about 30 BC to the early 18th century. Other timekeeping devices were being developed during this period, but they were complex, large, or expensive. It wasn't until the early 1700s that affordable clocks became available, making the sundial the only practical timekeeping device used by the masses for thousands of years.

Sundials have two basic parts: the dial and the gnomon. The time of day is indicated by how a shadow is cast by a gnomon upon the dial, a fixed object. Often, sundials have philosophical inscriptions, called sundial quotations. Some of my favorite are "Be careful that the light does not fail you during the day"; "Look in my shadow, you will see your life"; "Each one wounds, the last one kills"; "I know mine hour, dost thou know mine?"; "Time conquers all"; and "The sun shines for all."

A sundial should be placed in a spot that provides full sun. In order to be accurate, the dial should be level, and the gnomon should point toward celestial north. A simple way of finding celestial north is to adjust the dial at noon until the shadow of the gnomon points to the noon mark on the dial. Since sundials tell sun time, and mechanical clocks measure mean solar time, or standardized Greenwich Mean Time, sundial time will differ from our clocks and watches by varying degrees, depending on the distance you are from a standard meridian.

Partly because sundials are only useful on sunny days (not cloudy ones or at night), another method of telling time was sure to supersede it. Thus, clocks and watches were invented. Early watches were extremely unreliable, though, and, for some time, it was still necessary to keep a sundial to adjust time.

Although we have an array of precision timepieces at our disposal, it seems the trusty sundial has not lost its charm. Today, it is valued more for its aesthetic qualities and tradition than for its accuracy. Perhaps because the sundial demonstrates the passage of time without itself moving, its appeal is somehow connected to its simplicity. Sundials are easily constructed—and require no moving parts or repair.

Sundials are lovely when placed in the natural world they monitor and are a logical choice for garden ornaments. True, a sundial of your own construction, no matter how expertly put together, will never achieve the accuracy of your trusty wristwatch. But who among us is concerned with exact time when we work or relax in our garden?

REFLECTIVE STAR PLAQUE

DESIGNER: **Janice Rieves**

*P*ieces of broken mirror need not bring you bad luck in the garden. Indeed, shards of mirror will reflect colorful blooms during the day (doubling their impact) and cast a magical glimmer in the moonlight. A star-shaped plaque is particularly stunning at night when placed above a shimmery pool of water, though you can use this mold-making technique to create a variety of shapes.

GARDENER'S
TIP   *Don't be afraid to use unusual items as garden decorations. Learn to consider the potential of objects in your storage shed or at flea markets for containers and garden sculptures, such as wheelbarrows, pots, old washing tubs, crates, dilapidated furniture, and so forth.*

Materials and Tools

1-inch-thick (2.5-cm) piece of
   blue board insulation,
   2 x 2 feet (.6 x .6 m)

Clear contact paper

Piece of plywood (with dimensions
   at least 2 inches [5 cm] larger
   than the piece of insulation)

Mirror pieces, cut into triangular
   or square pieces (see step 5)

Large screw

5-inch (12.5-cm) length of twisted
   picture-hanging wire

Plaster of Paris, 2-pound (908-g)
   container

Serrated utility knife

Wide transparent tape

Glass cutters

Safety glasses, a dust mask,
   and gloves

Bucket

Fine sandpaper (optional)

Instructions

1 Use a serrated utility knife to cut a star shape out of the middle of the square piece of blue board insulation. Make sure there are at least 2 to 3 inches (5 to 7.5 cm) of board around the edges of the star. Remove star shape from the center of the insulation. You will use the square piece of insulation (with the star shape cut out of the center) as the mold. Seal the edges of the star with pieces of wide transparent tape.

2 Cut a piece of clear contact paper so that the edges of the contact paper extend 2 to 3 inches (5 to 7.5 cm) beyond the points of the star.

3 With a knife, cut from one tip of the star to the outer edge of the insulation. (This will aid in releasing the star from the mold, but will not ruin the mold.)

4 Peel the contact paper from the clear backing film, then lay the clear film on a piece of plywood with the sticky side up. Center star on top of film. You should now have a mold that consists of a piece of plywood, a layer of sticky paper (facing up), and a piece of insulation with a star-shaped center.

5 Make square or triangular mirror pieces by cutting strips of mirror, scoring, then cutting small pieces. (Wear safety glasses, a dust mask, and gloves for this step.)

6 Begin laying mirror pieces, face down, on the sticky contact paper, leaving at least ⅛ inch (.3 cm) between pieces. Press pieces down firmly to assure good contact.

7 Twist the ends of the 5-inch (12.5-cm) length of twisted picture-hanging wire around both ends of the large screw to make a hanger.

8 Mix the plaster with water in a bucket according to the manufacturer's instructions. At this point, you will need to work quickly before the plaster sets up. Pour the plaster into the mold slowly and evenly until it has reached the top lip of the mold. Press the screw into the plaster at the hanging point, leaving the wire loop exposed. Allow the plaster to cure for at least 24 hours.

9 To release the star from the mold, pull the mold apart slightly at the cut point (see step 3). Run a sharp knife around the edges of the mold to help loosen the plaster from the mold.

10 If the edges of the star come out rough, they can easily be sanded smooth with fine sandpaper.

GARDEN GAZING MIRROR

DESIGNER: **Susan Kinney**

Y̱ou've probably seen gazing balls for sale at upscale garden supply stores—they are among the most pricey garden ornaments. This moss-rimmed mirror is a reflective decoration of another kind that will double your view of a particularly enchanting garden spot or add light to a shady area of the garden. We've found these mirrors are particularly attractive to cats, who enjoy gazing at themselves on warm summer days.

Materials and Tools

Mirror, preferably one without a frame

Waterproof exterior-grade adhesive or silicone glue

Dried moss (amount will vary, depending on the size of the mirror)

Dried flowers (optional)

Instructions

1 Examine your garden for a pleasing location or a spot where you would like to have a little extra sparkle. Pick out a mirror shape (square, rectangular, or circular) and size that best suits the spot you have chosen. Decide whether you will hang your mirror, dig it into the ground, or prop it on the ground.

2 Glue bunches of moss around the edges of the mirror. Attach dried flowers as well, if desired. Use embellishment to make your gazing mirror as simple or as elaborate as you wish.

3 If you would like your mirror to be dug into the ground, leave the bottom side uncovered. If you would like to hang the mirror or lean it against a tree (as we've done here) or a large pot, decorate all four sides.

VERDIGRIS WIND CHIMES

$\mathbb{T}$his is a great project for the ecologically minded, since many of the materials, such as a CD case, a faucet knob, and a pot top, can be recycled from discarded household items. Though these items are made from a variety of substances (wood, plastic, and metal), they are easily given the uniform appearance of weathered metal by sponging on paint in a variety of colors.

Materials and Tools

10 feet (3 m) ¾-inch-diameter (2-cm) electrical metal tubing (EMT), available at hardware stores (chimes)

Lacquer thinner (optional)

Plastic compact disc case (wind vane)

Plastic twist-knob-style bathroom faucet handle, 2 to 3 inches (5 to 7.5 cm) in diameter (clapper)

Cooking-pot lid, approximately 7 inches (18 cm) in diameter, with knob removed (upper support)

S-hook or metal ring

Strong nylon cord, about ¹⁄₁₆ inch (2 mm) in diameter

Nut or washer (optional)

Black exterior metal primer

Enamel paint: green, white, and black

Hacksaw or heavy-duty metal tubing cutter

Flat metal file

Electric drill with ⅛-inch (.3-cm) bit and countersink bit

Scissors

Natural sponge

Feather

Spray polyurethane

DESIGNERS: **Bart Hopkin** (WIND CHIMES) AND **Sharon Trammel** (DECORATIVE PAINTING)

Instructions

1 Use a hacksaw or a heavy-duty metal tubing cutter to cut the metal tubing into four pieces: one 18 inches (45.8 cm) long, one 16½ inches (41.8 cm) long, one 15½ inches (39.7 cm) long, and one 14⅛ inches (36.2 cm) long. Use a metal file to clean up cut metal edges. If the metal tubing has printed markings or sticky paper labels on the surface, remove with lacquer thinner.

2 With a ⅛-inch (.3-cm) drill bit, drill a hole through each tube: 4 inches (10 cm) down from one end on the longest tube, 3½ inches (9 cm) down on the next longest tube, 3¼ inches (8.7 cm) down on the next longest tube, and 3 inches (8 cm) down on the shortest tube. Next, use the countersink bit to slightly bevel the hole edges to reduce the wear on the support cord.

3 Remove the compact disc and any paper from the case. Drill a ⅛-inch (.3-cm) hole at the center of the heavier, hinged side of the case, near the edge of the case. (The case should be held down firmly all around when you do this, or it will run up the bit when the bit breaks through and possibly fracture the plastic.)

4 Drill a ⅛-inch (.3-cm) hole vertically through the center of the faucet handle; this will be the clapper.

5 Place the clapper in the middle of the inside of the pot lid and trace around it with a marker. Mark four equally spaced locations around the pot lid, each 1½ inches (4 cm) from the outline of the clapper. Drill four holes on the lid, using these markings as a guide.

6 Cut four 18-inch (45.5-cm) lengths of cord and knot one end of each piece of cord with a triple knot. Run the cord for the first chime down through the first hole, through the chime, then back up through the second hole; for the second chime run the new cord down through the second hole, through the second chime, back up through the third hole. Continue this process with the other two chimes. The end of the cord for the fourth chime will come back up through the first hole to complete the circle. All four chimes should hang so that the centers of each chime is at the same level as the others. Thus, the top of the longest one will be the highest—an inch (2.5 cm) or so below the lid—and the other chimes will hang lower. Knot the end of the cord, carefully locating the knot so that the chimes hang at the correct height. Trim off any excess cord.

7 Cut a 30-inch (76-cm) piece of cord and triple knot one end. If the center hole (where the knob was) in the pot lid is very large, tie the cord through a nut or a washer to prevent the knot from slipping through. Pull the cord through the center hole in the lid from above. Run it through the hole in the clapper (the faucet handle). Tie a knot below the clapper in the cord so that when the clapper drops down against the knot, it hangs at the chimes' vertical midpoint. Run the remaining end of the cord through the hole in the CD case, then tie it so that it hangs just below the lower end of the longest chime. Trim off any excess cord.

8 Cut four 12-inch (30.5-cm) pieces of cord and triple knot one end of each. Pull the cord up through the four holes in the lid from underneath. (This will be the third of three cords that will pass through these holes, so it will be a snug fit.) Tie the opposite ends of the cords to the S-hook or metal ring, so that the lid hangs level. (You may have to retie the cord several times to get the lengths correct for a level hang.) Trim off excess cord.

9 Hang the wind chimes in an easily accessible spot for painting. First, paint the entire surface of all the parts with black spray primer. Allow primer to dry thoroughly.

10 Mix together one part green paint, one part white paint, and a small amount of black paint. Sponge paint mixture randomly over the surface of the wind chimes.

11 Add white to the paint mixture to create a lighter color and sponge this mixture over the wind chimes as well, blending paint in some areas as desired.

12 Use a feather that has been dipped in white paint to create vein marks on the chimes. Allow paint to dry thoroughly.

13 Spray clear polyurethane finish over the entire surface of the wind chimes.

Keeyla Meadows is a sculptor, painter, ceramicist, and landscape designer who creates gardens that are works of art. Her passion for flowers is the inspiration for her colorful garden ornaments.

TOP LEFT: WOMAN WITH LEMON TREE
Glazed ceramic
PHOTO: Keeyla Meadows

TOP RIGHT: BUTTERFLY BENCH GARDEN
Painted steel (bench)
PHOTO: Keeyla Meadows

BOTTOM LEFT: BUTTERFLY BENCH
Painted steel
PHOTO: Keeyla Meadows

BOTTOM RIGHT: GARDEN POT WITH
GREEN LEAF (LEFT) AND GARDEN POT
WITH POPPY PODS (RIGHT)
Glazed ceramic (pots) and steel (trellis)
PHOTO: Keeyla Meadows

COPPER-PIPING
CANDLE HOLDER

This striking candle holder is made by simply cutting pipe to various lengths, attaching the pieces with t-connectors and adhesive, and suspending a candle with copper wire. Refer to page 86 for instructions on making your own container candle.

DESIGNER: **Janice Rieves**

Materials and Tools

½-inch (1.5-cm) rigid copper piping, two 8-foot (2.5-m) lengths

Twelve ½-inch (1.5-cm) copper t-connectors

Eight ½-inch (1.5-cm) copper end caps

Flexible copper wire

Container candle with fluted lip

Spray lacquer or poly-urethane (optional)

Hand-held pipe cutter

Sandpaper (optional)

Plumber's adhesive or clear waterproof exterior-grade adhesive

Wire cutters

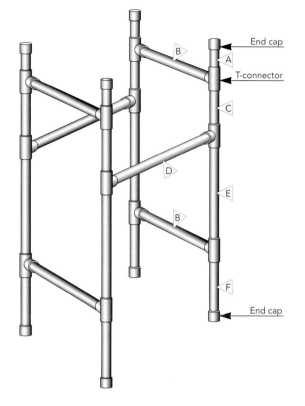

Instructions

1 Use a hand-held pipe cutter to cut the ½-inch (1.5-cm) copper piping to the following lengths: Four 2½-inch (6.5-cm) pieces (A), four 9-inch (23-cm) pieces (B), four 5-inch (12.5-cm) pieces (C), two 8½-inch (21.5-cm) pieces (D), four 20½-inch (52-cm) pieces (E), and four 5½-inch (14-cm) pieces (F). (See diagram.) If necessary, sand off any markings on the copper piping.

2 Attach pieces of pipe with t-connectors at the points shown in the diagram, securing with plumber's adhesive or clear waterproof exterior-grade adhesive.

3 Attach end caps (four on the top and four on the bottom) with plumber's adhesive or clear waterproof exterior-grade adhesive. Allow at least 24 hours for adhesive to dry.

4 The candle is held in place with two pieces of copper wire that fit under the neck of the fluted container and wrap around the copper posts of the holder (see photograph). The length of copper wire you will need will depend on the candle you have chosen. Use wire cutters to cut two pieces of copper wire to the desired length. Wrap each end of one wire around the posts on one side of the holder three or four times and place the loop of wire around the neck of the candle container. Repeat this process with the remaining wire on the other two copper posts. Adjust wires as needed so that candle sits level.

5 If you do not want the candle holder to turn green with age (verdigris), apply a coat of spray lacquer or polyurethane to the entire surface of the candle holder.

Chapter 6

*More
Fabulous
Accents*

LIVING WREATHS

Wreaths made from living materials make stunning garden decorations throughout the season. And you can replace the plants as the seasons change—pansies in the spring, impatiens in the summer, and hardy herbs in the fall and winter. Be sure you choose plants that require the same amount of light (all sun-loving, all shade-loving, and so forth). When placed face-up on a garden table, these wreaths also make gorgeous centerpieces.

Materials and Tools

(for a 24-inch [61-cm] wreath)

Selection of living plants (see instructions and quantities in step 5)

Sphagnum or sheet moss, enough to cover wreath form

Concave wire wreath form (available at garden centers)

High-quality potting mix

Timed-release fertilizer

Large bucket or sink

Instructions

1 Water all the plants you will be using for the wreath, then thoroughly soak the sphagnum or sheet moss in water until it is completely wet.

2 Working on a level surface, line the inside of the back of the wreath form with moss. Wring out the moss—handful by handful—and pack it against the edges of the form, allowing some moss to drape over the sides of the wreath form. Make sure there are no gaps where the soil can escape.

3 Mix together soil and timed-release potting soil (following the manufacturer's instructions) in a large bucket or sink and fill the moss-lined form with the mixture.

4 Attach the top of the wire frame to the bottom. It is important to do this before putting the plants in the frame so that the plants do not get crushed. An exception to this is the variegated ivy on the impatiens wreath (see step 5), which should be planted before the frame is closed.

5 Break open the root balls of the plants you intend to use and shake off excess soil. (See below for specific planting instructions.) Arrange the plants around the wreath to create a pleasing balance of color and texture. Use plants in sets of threes to create an appealing triangular or star-shaped effect. Balance colors and textures on opposite sides of the wreath and make the floral composition as full and interesting as possible.

To make the pink and blue wreath (left), we've used a selection of annuals, such as pink ivy geraniums, blue and white lobelia, licorice plant, pink verbena, bacopa, ivy, and purple million bells (miniature petunias). (The exact number of each will vary, depending on the degree of fullness you want your wreath to have.)

To make the impatiens wreath (see page 108), the designer used about 15 plants each impatiens and variegated ivy. Plant ivy before you close the wreath base, spacing evenly, then fill in with impatiens after the form is secure. Alternate colors and spacing to create visual interest.

ESIGNER: **Alice Belz**

DESIGNER: **Mardi Letson**

6 Cover the roots of each plant with soil. This can be tricky, since, at this point, there is very little space in the wreath form.

7 Carefully pack small pieces of moss between plants, tucking the moss under the wire in spots to secure. Be sure to position the moss on the sides close enough to the moss on top so that the soil will not spill out when the wreath is watered.

8 It is a good idea to leave the living wreath lying flat for a few days so the plants will have a chance to establish themselves. Water the wreath lightly each day. When the plants have passed the initial transplant shock (several days), hang the wreath in your garden.

9 Prune the plants as needed to encourage them to keep the form of the wreath, and water frequently. You can overwinter the living wreath by placing it in a shallow hole in the ground.

GARDENER'S
TIP   *If your living wreath will hang on a wooden surface, either tack a piece of plastic to the wood or place a piece of floral foam between the door and the wreath so that the water can drain.*

GARDEN JOURNAL

DESIGNER: **Mardi Letson**

A journal is a great way for gardeners to record plantings, flower names, and other useful planting information—or to scribble a garden-inspired poem or sketch. If you plan to leave your journal outside or if you anticipate keeping it with you in the garden, choose water-resistant fabric or sturdy paper for the cover and spray the outer surface with weather-resistant spray.

Materials and Tools

Purchased journal

Handmade cover paper, (amount will vary, depending on the size of the journal)

Rawhide shoelace

Scissors

Fine ballpoint pen

Small paintbrush

White craft glue

Rolling pin

Wax paper

Instructions

1. Cut paper to a rectangular size that will cover the journal you've chosen (including spine), plus an additional 1 inch (2.5 cm) on each side.

2. Using a fine ballpoint pen, lightly draw a straight line 1 inch (2.5 cm) in from the bottom on the underside of the paper. Make a small mark at the midpoint of the line and another mark directly above it, approximately 1 inch (2.5 cm) from the top. These marks will help you align the book on the paper.

3. Using a small paintbrush, spread a thin, even layer of craft glue on the underside of the paper. Align the middle of the spine with the marked midpoint. Use the marks to align the book in a straight line on the paper.

4. Carefully attach the front cover, roll the book over to press the paper to the spine, then attach the paper to the back cover. Use a rolling pin to smooth.

5 To finish corners, fold in both corners on the front side, then carefully fold over the paper on the short side. Using scissors, make two small, straight incisions where the inside front cover meets the spine. The length of the incision should be just long enough to allow you to fold the bottom and top of the paper neatly over the front cover. Repeat step 5 with the back cover. Two small tabs of paper will remain at the spine. Trim them so they can be tucked into the spine area.

6 Cut shoelaces to the desired length and glue them in place on the inside of each cover about one third of the way down from the top of the journal. The end of each shoelace should extend almost to the spine. Glue a small piece of scrap paper over the shoelace to secure.

7 Cut two pieces of paper to the exact size of the inside cover plus the front page. Spread glue on the cover and the page, and press pieces of paper in place. Allow to dry for several seconds, then use a rolling pin to smooth.

8 Insert a piece of wax paper between the front cover and the front page of the book, wrap around the outside, and insert wax paper between the back cover and the last page of the book. Allow book to dry under pressure. The wax paper will keep the pages from sticking together as the glue dries.

WHIMSICAL SUN FACE

DESIGNER:
Pamella Wilson

Every garden has a space that needs a little extra cheer—a plain door, a bare shed wall, or a wooden fence post. This charming clay sunshine with a smiling countenance may also be just the right touch for a flowerless spot (possibly a shady area). And since it's made with clay that is baked in your home oven, it is a much easier project than you may think.

Materials and Tools

1 pound (454 g) terra-cotta oven clay

Rawhide strip

Flat board to use as work surface

Pillowcase

Rolling pin

Plate

Pencil

Newsprint

Wooden clay tools (optional)

Kitchen knife or other pointed tool

Chopstick

Plastic

GARDENER'S TIP *Position garden wall decorations and hanging baskets at eye level to achieve the most dramatic and pleasing visual effect.*

Instructions

1 Cover board with a pillowcase. Use the rolling pin to roll out oven clay on board into a 10- to 12-inch (25.5- to 30.5-cm) diameter circle with a ¼- to ½-inch (.5- to 1.5-cm) thickness.

2 Draw a smaller 6- to 8-inch (15- to 20.5-cm) circle inside the larger circle by tracing around a plate with a pencil. Use the pencil to lightly draw a simple face (eyes, nose, and mouth) within the small circle.

3 Carefully lift up slab and place scrunched-up newsprint under face where forehead, cheeks, nose, and chin will be. Gently set slab back down.

4 Continue to form face with your fingers and any other clay tools you may have. Use the kitchen knife or another sharp, pointed tool to make small dots in a design around the outside of the face, along the bottom, and above the eyes.

5 Push clay down around the circle and cut out a jagged design around the edge with a knife. Use a chopstick to make holes on each side of the sun face for hanging.

6 The clay will need to dry out slowly before it is baked to prevent cracking. Cover finished sun face with plastic and let stand for one day. Loosen plastic, but don't uncover, and again let stand for one day. The next day, uncover the sun face completely in the morning; in the evening, flip the piece over and loosely cover with plastic. Uncover the plastic the next day, and check the temperature of the clay by putting it up to your face. The clay should be at room temperature before baking; if either side of the clay is cold to the touch, it is not ready to bake. (The designer let this sun face dry for four days, alternating sides each day.)

7 When the sun face is ready (see step 6), bake according to manufacturer's instructions.

8 String rawhide strip through the premade holes in the sun face and tie knots in the ends of the strip.

Garden paths & walkways

WHETHER it's a serpentine gravel path wending its way through a lush wildflower garden or a formal blue slate walkway flanked by giant boxwoods, pathways can be a wonderful design feature for any garden. Paths and walkways encourage people to stroll through a garden (thus, allowing them to enjoy it) and can be used to direct traffic to the most appealing areas. When well planned, pathways can add architectural interest, charm, and order to almost any garden setting.

When planning a pathway, consider the mood you have established (or want to establish) in your garden; the materials you choose should complement your chosen style. There's a wide variety of possibilities: cement, gravel, clay, brick, quarry tile, aggregate, flagstone, and sand are only a few of the possibilities.

A straight, paved path goes well with a more formal garden. A footpath made of simple stepping stones is a nice addition to a casual, untamed area of the garden. Invest in one or two accent stones (carved or imprinted with designs) to place in strategic areas of the garden; these are more expensive than plain stones, but can have a powerful impact. Winding walkways and paths with staggered walking patterns work well because they encourage the stroller to go slowly and examine the plants as they pass.

Wood rounds make nice stepping spots and shredded bark creates a woodland feel. Found materials make great paths, as demonstrated in the photograph at right (center); this gardener used an assortment of flat scrap metal—boiler plates and manhole covers, for example—to create a striking and unique pathway. If you like the formal look of brick, but want a more rustic path, purchase old red brick pavers. Inexpensive plastic guides are also available that help align bricks for a more formal, ordered walkway.

Molds can be purchased at home and garden supply centers that allow you to make cobblestone-like stones for patios, walkways, or paths. Concrete steppers can offer just the right touch to small garden spaces. Simple stones can be created easily by pouring cement into any makeshift mold (plastic planter bases work well) then pressing leaves, rocks, seashells, or a variety of other materials into the wet cement.

Before you begin, consider the amount of materials you will need to complete your entire pathway, and visit your local building supply center to compare prices and availability. A long pathway may necessitate some economizing. You will also need to consider maintenance. A brick pathway in a damp, shady spot may need a wash of bleach periodically to discourage the growth of slippery moss. Or you may opt for a simple path of gravel or pebbles, which is essentially maintenance-free.

Place benches and seating along paths where scented flowers are concentrated and at dead-ends. Scented flowers and herbs—such as scented geraniums, rosemary, mint, and lavender—are best placed along paths where visitors will brush against the leaves to release the aroma. Planting creeping plants and lush ground covers in crevices between steppers gives a garden an abundant, wild feel. Try creeping thyme, baby's tears, or dwarf cypress. Plant short- to medium-sized flowers and foliage along the path approximately 2 feet (.6 m) from the edge to create borders. (Do not plant too close to the path as the plants will need room to expand and mature.)

When planning your pathway, it is best to consider existing travel patterns, then make changes as needed. Position stepping stones where your feet naturally fall. If you plan to have two people walking together on your walkway, make it at least 4 feet (1.2 m) wide; otherwise, 3 feet (.9 m) should be plenty of room.

DESIGN: **Christopher Mello**

A path should be at least 2 feet (.6 m) away from a hedge, wall, or any other tall structure. You may also want to broaden the path slightly at curves.

Another way to make your garden more accessible and to create a sense of movement is to create steps. This makes sense particularly when the grade is greater than ten percent and a change of elevation is in order. Steps can be made out of the same materials as paths and walkways, though you need to take more care that the surfaces are sturdy.

If you plan to use pavers, bricks, or other hard-surface materials, you must first establish a base of sand at least 2 inches (5 cm) thick. (If you live in an especially cold climate, you might want to consider laying 2 to 4 inches [5 to 10 cm] of gravel underneath the sand.) Pay special attention to how the water will drain. Do not create spaces in which water will easily collect, rather raise the middle of the path slightly.

Lighting may also be a consideration, depending on the location of your pathway (see page 87). Path lighting may be necessary for practical purposes, but it can also be used to create a mood at night. Soft lighting along the edge of the path will serve to illuminate the flowers and foliage as well as to lead walkers through the garden.

DESIGN: **Keeyla Meadows**

ROCKS IN BLOOM

DESIGNER: **Laura Dawn Roberson**

Most of us are experienced rock painters, since this activity is a favorite among camp counselors and schoolteachers. Here's a sophisticated (and garden-oriented) take that offers limitless creative expression. In winter, bring the rocks inside to create a gorgeous decorative element—and a fond reminder of your spring and summer blooms.

GARDENER'S TIP *Painted rocks make super doorstops (possibly for a barn or garden shed), stepping stones, or garden decorations for areas without many flowers.*

Materials and Tools

Assorted rocks in a variety of sizes and shapes

Pencil (with dark lead)

Multipurpose latex paint in assorted colors

Sponge or stiff brush

Paintbrushes in assorted sizes

Exterior clear polyurethane spray

Instructions

1 Clean rock thoroughly with a sponge or a stiff brush (depending on how dirty it is) that has been dipped in water. Allow to dry thoroughly.

2 Sketch your chosen design on the rock with a pencil; you will need a pencil with dark lead, since lighter pencils may not show up. Gardening magazines and floral design books are great sources for flower designs—but don't forget the plants in your own garden!

3 When you are pleased with the design (feel free to erase and adjust as long as necessary), brush on latex paint to color the flowers. Mix color to achieve nonbasic colors, such as purples, oranges, and greens, as well as varying shades of blue, yellow, and red. Also, dilute paint with water, if desired.

4 When the rock is completely dry, spray on at least three coats of polyurethane to provide extra protection and a smooth, even, and more finished look.

HOUSE NUMBER

I dentify your house number and display a beautiful mosaic design at once with this delightful creation—or make a similar decoration that features any other motif, such as a leaf, a flower, or a bird.

DESIGNER: **Terry Taylor**

Materials and Tools

Terra-cotta chimney flue pipe

An assortment of ceramic plates or tiles

Cement mortar

Sanded floor grout

Permanent marker or other marking tool

Tile nippers

Safety glasses

Mixing containers for mortar and grout

Plastic (to cover work space)

Small disposable palette knife or picnic knife

Polyethylene packing sheet foam

Latex gloves

Barely damp sponge or lint-free rags (optional)

Protective sealant (optional)

Instructions

1 Begin by drawing your house number (or any other design motif) to size on one or more sides of the flue pipe with a permanent marker or other marking tool.

2 Use tile nippers to break plates into irregular pieces. Break them into small, flattish pieces and set them aside. *Note:* Always wear safety glasses when breaking/nipping plates with tile nippers! Determine which colors of ceramic you would like to use in which areas of the design.

3 Mix a small batch of cement mortar according to the manufacturer's instructions, allowing it to cure briefly as directed. Start with about ⅓ cup (80 ml) of water and mix the dry mortar into the water until you achieve the consistency of thick mud.

4 Lay your flue pipe on its side to work on one side at a time. Use a disposable knife to apply a small amount of mortar to each tile piece, and set it in place. Fill in the outlined design with tiles. You may wish to use one color for the number and a contrasting color for the outline. Working on one side at a time, cover the flue with broken plate and tile pieces. Use tile nippers to trim pieces to fit, if necessary. Allow each side to dry overnight before covering the next side.

5 Cover your work surface with plastic before grouting. Place the finished flue tile upright for the grouting process. Mix the sanded floor grout according the manufacturer's instructions. Use about ¼ to ½ cup (60 to 120 ml) of clean water and add the grout to achieve a consistency of cake frosting. You may have to mix an additional batch to completely grout the tile.

6 Use a small square of polyethylene foam to apply the grout to the flu pipe. (Wear latex gloves to protect your hands.) Work the grout into the spaces between your plate pieces. Cover the entire pipe in this manner. After about 15 minutes, begin removing excess grout and grout haze with clean pieces of the foam, a barely damp sponge, or lint-free rags.

7 Allow the house number to dry following the manufacturer's instructions. If you wish, you may give your pipe additional protection from the freeze/thaw cycle of winter by coating it inside and out with a protective sealant compatible with the grout. Further protection is provided by placing the tile on gravel or elevating it slightly off the ground to provide drainage.

ARTIST'S GALLERY *Lyman Whitaker*

Lyman Whitaker creates kinetic wind sculptures in his Utah studio and markets them in fine art galleries around the United States. Though creating art that interacts with wind is his main focus, Whitaker's larger body of work is varied and ranges from traditional bronzes to fountains to jewelry.

WIND FOREST, 1988
Steel, stainless steel, copper
PHOTO: Stacy L. Christensen

STAR DANCER, 1993
Steel, stainless steel, copper
PHOTO: Stacy L. Christensen

SINGLE HELIX, 1995
Steel, stainless steel, copper
PHOTO: Stacy L. Christensen

DOUBLE DANCER, 1995
Steel, stainless steel, copper
PHOTO: Stacy L. Christensen

Garden junk

Do YOU find it impossible to pass a yard sale without a quick peek? Do you slam on your brakes and turn the car around, your heart racing, just for the pleasure of pilfering through someone else's junk? If you are a gardener and a junker, you're doubly blessed (or cursed, depending on your perspective). Collecting junk—or *salvage*, as it is known to those on the in—and turning your loot into unique garden ornaments has become a passion for many gardeners.

Christopher Mello, avid gardener and professional designer, is a master at recycling salvage into garden art. In his riverside studio, he transforms scrap metal into garden containers and decorations. Metal garden ornaments are the rage among garden artists, as you can see from our Artist's Gallery throughout this book. Metal decorations are easy to make with an assortment of found items (see bottom right photograph on page 119). Mello suggests searching out pieces of metal at salvage yards and junk stores. Look for old farm equipment—the parts often make great garden sculpture. Ask your local antique dealers for metal items (though they're likely to charge more than through a salvage yard).

ABOVE: An assortment of found metal objects used in the garden

RIGHT: Three chicken feeders filled with various stages of plantings

Mello points out that there is much potential for using salvage as garden containers and planters. Old shoe-shining boxes, wire baskets, paint-chipped pails, as well as previously owned crates, teapots, flower boxes, feed buckets, bins, chimney pots, and even unidentifiable found objects make unique (and enduring) containers. As shown in the photograph on the bottom of page 118, Mello recycled chicken feeders into striking succulent planters and seedling troughs. He also transformed a small metal wood stove into a one-of-a-kind garden container (see page 121). Make sure any potential container will hold soil and has adequate drainage. Succulent dishes require a shallow opening.

The tops of oil drums and even 5-gallon buckets make terrific birdbaths or water garden planters. An old sink, a bucket, or even a bowl found at a thrift store can make a charming birdbath. In his garden, Mello has arranged an assortment of worn-out boots on a rusty glider to create a whimsical presentation (see photograph, top). The boots have built-in holes for water drainage; they were simply filled with soil and planted with draught-tolerant plants. (Birds will also nest in boots.)

ABOVE: Leather boots are packed with dirt and planted, then perched on an old glider under the shade of weeping willow.

FAR LEFT: A cracked wash bowl half buried at the edge of a flower garden makes a perfect watering hole for squirrels and birds.

LEFT: A bounty of garden potential. Industrial gears, cams, and casings are arranged along a path tiled with spiral staircase steps in the yard of Christopher Mello's studio.

A concrete laundry sink is rescued from the dump and put to good use as an outdoor aquatic garden. Concrete and soapstone sinks work best outdoors, because their surface will age beautifully. Raised off the ground a few inches for drainage, sinks are also perfect for fountains and miniature fish ponds.

A pair of rusty chairs makes a charming garden seating area. See page 16 for instructions for making the distressed planter shown behind the small chair.

When searching for garden goodies, don't instantly write off pieces as useless—sometimes a clever eye can see beyond the disrepair. Pieces of old fencing or shutters can be transformed into arbors or trellises or can be attached to a wall to create an ideal base for creeping plants and vines. Watering cans (especially galvanized ones) are treasures, but be careful: Antique dealers sell them for a small fortune. They make great garden ornaments and containers—even if they are not functional. (If you plan to use a watering can for its intended purpose, though, check for leaks before you buy it.)

Embellishing your garden space with salvage furniture is an inexpensive way to achieve a unique decorative effect. Wrought-iron garden chairs, wooden benches, and metal stools are particularly good finds. Aged tables make excellent potting benches and storage areas. Metal pot holders, planters, and plant stands are common and usually can be had for very little money—and they can be either stripped down and given a fresh coat of paint or left as is. (True junkers learn to appreciate rusty metal and peeling paint and would not dare disrupt the aging process.) Wicker furniture, though it does not remain functional when left outdoors, make a charming surface for potted plants.

My husband is convinced that the most well-made tools are vintage and surely, in many cases, that's true. There's also the satisfaction of knowing your equipment has been put to use in another garden and has stood the test of time. Trowels, hoes, rakes, shovels, pruning shears, and such can often be spotted at markets and sales. Be careful not to be charmed by tools that can't be repaired, unless you want the item just for decorative purposes.

There are infinite possibilities when it comes to making use of found junk in the garden. A rickety child's wagon or a rusted garden cart may be just what you need to transport bulbs and soil and tools around your garden. A worn wicker basket may be ideal for carrying flowers and vegetables. And since you have very little investment in these items, they can be left out in the elements without guilt. An old wooden box is a perfect storage compartment for seed packets and garden gloves. Broken-down wheelbarrows make great vessels for clusters of summer annuals or herbs. Straw hats with holes can adorn a shed door or the seat of a garden chair

Here's a tip: Always take along cash (preferably small bills and lots of change) on your junking jaunts. Some dealers don't take anything else, and often the prices are so low—50 cents or a dollar—that a few coins or bills are all that stand between you, that great find, and a fabulous garden ornament.

TOP OF PAGE: Christopher Mello's garden features rustic birdbaths made from found metal disks.

LEFT: A variety of garden structures can be built from planks of discarded wood. See page 22 for instructions for making this garden storage box.

ABOVE: Two unique garden objects: A pot-bellied wood stove that has been transformed into a container for herbs and succulents (left) and a plant stand made by welding together an assortment of metal pieces (right).

MOSAIC STEPPING STONES

Some crafters are addicted to searching out ceramic plates for use in projects, such as these great garden stepping stones. Indeed such plates can be had for very little money at flea markets, tag sales, and thrift stores. If you don't catch the bug, however, scrap ceramic tiles can also be used for this project.

Materials and Tools

Concrete stepping stone

An assortment of ceramic plates

Cement mortar

Sanded floor grout

Tile nippers

Safety glasses

Mixing containers for mortar and grout

Small disposable palette knife or picnic knife

Plastic (to cover work space)

Polyethylene packing sheet foam

Rubber or latex gloves

Barely damp sponge or lint-free rags (optional)

Protective sealant (optional)

Instructions

1 Use tile nippers to cut large pieces from the rims of the chosen plates. You do not need to keep the rim edges of the plates intact, but you will need these pieces to fill spaces between the circles. (This designer used the raised edge of the back of the plate as a design motif.) Trim as many plates as you wish to create circles for your stone.

2 Place the circular pieces on the stepping stone, experiment with positioning, and determine whether you need more circles. Use the tile nippers to break the rim edges into pieces that will lay flat to fill in the space between the circles. Set pieces aside.

3 Mix a small batch of cement mortar according to the manufacturer's instructions, allowing it to cure briefly as directed. Start with about ⅓ cup (80 ml) of water and mix the dry mortar into the water until you achieve the consistency of thick mud.

4 Apply mortar to the stepping stone with a small disposable palette knife or picnic knife. Place the plate centers as desired on the stepping stone, then fill in between the circles with the smaller pieces. Use tile nippers to trim pieces to fit, if necessary. Allow the mortar to dry for at least 24 hours.

5 Cover your work surface with plastic before grouting. Mix the sanded floor grout according the manufacturer's instructions. Use about ¼ cup (60 ml) of clean water and add the grout to achieve a consistency of cake frosting.

6 Use a small square of polyethylene foam to apply the grout to the stepping stone. (Wear latex gloves to protect your hands.) Work the grout into the spaces between the plate pieces. Cover the entire stone in this manner. After about 15 minutes, begin removing excess grout and grout haze with clean pieces of the foam, a barely damp sponge, or lint-free rags.

7 Allow the stepping stone to dry as directed in the manufacturer's instructions. If you wish, you may give the stepping stone additional protection by coating it with a protective sealant compatible with the grout. Give your stepping stones protection from the freeze/thaw cycle of winter by bringing them indoors

SQUIRMY GARDEN WORM

This delightful creature is sure to be a friendly addition to any child's garden spot. And it's a great rainy-day project that will also educate kids about the benefits many of nature's creatures have on the garden. All of the materials are available at the local hardware store or home center. The plastic globe can be found in the lighting section among the fixtures, but you can use any round object that will fit securely into the pipe collar and hold up to outdoor conditions.

Materials and Tools

One 6- to 8-inch (15- to 20-cm) diameter plastic globe

Four 45° PVC elbows, 4 inches (10 cm) in diameter

One 90° PVC elbow, 4 inches (10 cm) in diameter

One 4-inch (10-cm) PVC cap

All-purpose cement for PVC plumbing

Exterior spray latex paint: green

Exterior latex paint: blue and white

Pencil and paper

Scissors

Masking tape

Paintbrush

DESIGNER (AND POET): **Heather Smith**

Worm, worm, you do delight
The garden with your appetite
For leaves and peels and insect wings
You break these down for growing things.
And while you eat
You also squirm,
Which keeps my soil from getting firm.
So thanks for all the good you give
To help my flowers and vegetables live.

Instructions

1 Begin by spraying the plastic globe and each section of pipe, including the rims, with three coats of green exterior latex paint. Allow paint to dry thoroughly between coats.

2 Set the open end of the globe into the collar of one of the 45° elbows to check for fit and placement.

3 Draw worm eyes on paper (see photograph). Cut out the eyes and use masking tape to secure the eyes to the globe.

4 When the eyes are positioned on the globe, trace onto the globe around the outer edges of the eyes with a pencil and remove paper. Paint in the eyes with white and blue paint (or any other colors of your choice). If necessary, once the paint has dried, cover the eyes with masking tape (taking care to cover eye shapes exactly) and spray the entire globe with another layer of green paint. This will cover up any uneven edges or paint smudges around the eyes.

5 To attach the head (globe), apply all-purpose cement to the inside rim of the 45° elbow collar, then fit the globe into this end. Allow the cement to set according to manufacturer's instructions.

6 Assemble the remaining pieces so that one 45° elbow has a cap and the other two elbows are joined to each end of the 90° elbow to make an arch for the middle section (use the photograph as a guide). It is not necessary to use cement for these PVC parts, as they will fit together snugly.

7 Place the finished sections into the soil as shown, so that the worm appears to be crawling through the garden.

GARDENER'S TIP *Encourage exercise and an appreciation of nature in your children by planting a small garden just for them. Create a pathway with small stones and plant low-growing (nonpoisonous) flowers. Encourage the children to help tend the garden.*

Designers

ALICE BELZ just moved to St. Louis, Missouri, though she gained much of her gardening experience working at a garden center in her hometown in North Carolina. There, she developed a love for container gardening, annuals, herbs, and vegetables.

PAMELA BROWN is a professional candlemaker who owns and operates Mountain Lights, a candle and lighting shop in Asheville, North Carolina. In addition to her line of hand-dipped candles, she creates candle holders made from recycled products.

KATHLEEN BURKE started her own mural company while in college. Her painstaking work as a restorer of antique paintings is balanced by her love of creating faux finishes and decorative surfaces.

ROBIN CLARK lives in Asheville, North Carolina, where he and his wife, Helen, own and operate Robin's Wood, Ltd. They manufacture a variety of spectacular wooden outdoor products for people and wildlife.

JOEL COLE lives in Weaverville, North Carolina. He is an avid gardener and artist who draws most of the inspiration for his creative endeavors from his garden. He especially enjoys painting garden-themed murals.

JULIE ANNE EASON is a freelance writer and artist living in Bucksport, Maine. Though her talents and interests are various and widespread, she particularly enjoys crafting with beach glass. She also weaves and spins reproduction textiles for historic reenactments.

GAY GRIMSLEY is a decorative painter in Asheville, North Carolina, who specializes in faux finishes on walls and furniture. She loves to transform the ordinary into the extraordinary—to turn a simple piece into something fun, unusual, and unexpected.

BART HOPKIN is a designer and builder of acoustic musical instruments, and a student of world musical instruments. Since 1985 he has been publisher and editor of *Experimental Musical Instruments* (email: emi@windworld.com), and he has written several books on musical instruments and their construction.

DANA IRWIN is an art director at Lark Books who grabs every chance she can to garden in her yard with her two helpful canine companions, Parker (the path-maker) and Chou-Chou (the hole-digger).

SUSAN KINNEY was trained in formal art and is now a papermaker, potter, jeweler, and interior designer who lives in Asheville, North Carolina.

MARDI LETSON is a social worker who lives in Asheville, North Carolina, with her husband, Kellett, her son, Austin, and her dogs, Moses and Shelby. She creates gorgeous floral crafts and home decorative items in her basement studio.

CHRISTOPHER MELLO is a horticulturist by trade, though he prefers to call himself a gardener, and has expanded his expertise to include metal sculpture and floral design. He gained much of his experience on the grounds of the historic Biltmore Estate in his hometown of Asheville, North Carolina.

ANNE McCLOSKEY is an energetic freelance artist from Copley, Ohio, who generates new ideas for craft manufacturers and magazines around the country. Although she specializes in painting, Anne's favorite form of artwork involves experimentation with various forms of media.

TAMARA MILLER is a stay-home mom and crafter who lives in Hendersonville, North Carolina, with her son, Beck, and her husband, Jeff. Her crafting interests include making Santas and Christmas stockings, as well as projects that involve her son.

CAROL PARKS has enjoyed a lifetime love affair with sewing and gardening. She has written numerous sewing books, has had a career as a book editor, and is an accomplished bagpipe player. She lives in Asheville, North Carolina.

JANICE RIEVES creates unique pieces of art using recycled and salvaged materials. She lives on seven acres in rural Chatham County, North Carolina, with her husband, three children, cats, dogs, goats, and rabbits.

LAURA ROBERSON is an artist who is currently studying textile design in Philadelphia. Her stint at a floral shop inspired her to capture flowers and foliage on paper—and to create the gorgeous painted rocks featured in this book (see pages 114–15).

OLIVIER ROLLIN is a multimedia designer who studied industrial design at a commercial art school in Paris, France, before leaving his native country for the United States. After extensive travels around America, he settled in Asheville, North Carolina, where he thrives in a back-alley studio.

OWEN SAYLES lives in Asheville, North Carolina, where he enjoys gardening and working at two jobs; when he's not creating cement pots in his basement (see pages 20–21), he is a church youth director.

Gallery Artists

GLADYS SMITH works at Green Valley Wood Crafts in Leicester, North Carolina, where she uses her talents as a tole painter to embellish everything from barn wood to gourds.

HEATHER SMITH, editorial assistant at Lark Books, grew up on the coast of Maine, where she taught environmental education. She now enjoys crafting and exploring around her new home in the mountains of western North Carolina.

TERRY TAYLOR specializes in creating art for the garden using pique-assiette, or shard art, technique. Terry is known for his willingness to try any craft—and does a fabulous job at whatever he tries. He collects, creates, and carves from his home in Asheville, North Carolina.

KIM TIBBALS-THOMPSON resides in Waynesville, North Carolina. She is a frequent contributor to craft books and enjoys drawing, sewing, gardening, herbal crafting, and broom making. By day, she is a graphic designer.

SHARON TOMPKINS has literally worked from floor to ceiling and all points in between in her work as a decorative painter. She uses paint to transform everything from walls to flowerpots.

SHARON TRAMMEL lives atop Beaucatcher Mountain, a perch that rewards her daily with an inspiring view of downtown Asheville, North Carolina, where she teaches art classes at a local community college. She also paints murals on the walls and ceilings of a host of local restaurants and hospitals.

SKIP WADE indulges in the fascinations of wire creation only after fulfilling his obligations as a photo stylist in Asheville, North Carolina. In addition to whimsical wire work (see pages 24 and 26), he enjoys knitting, gardening, and reading.

PAMELLA WILSON lives in the mountains of North Carolina, where she is an accomplished potter and visual artist. She lists professional clowning among her former occupations, and is known for her wide range of crafting skills.

MELANIE WOODSON lives in Asheville, North Carolina, where she is a whiz crafter. Mosaics, polymer clay, painting, beadwork, needlepoint, knitting, metalwork, and stained glass are only a few of her many talents. When she's not creating something beautiful, she sings in a band.

STEFAN BONITZ (PAGE 91)
Steebo Designs
86 South Lexington Ave. (#4)
Asheville, NC 28801
www.circle.net/steebo

GARY CALDWELL (PAGE 19)
Mantis
5605 Wendell Road
Chapel Hill, NC 27514
(919) 408-6993

MARGARET DAHM (PAGE 41)
194 Edgewood Road
Asheville, NC 28804

IVY FLETCHER AND
PAT RIESENBURGER (PAGE 77)
RiesenFletcher YardWorks
600 5th Avenue North
Safety Harbor, FL 34695
(727) 726-0705

ARTHUR HIGGINS (PAGE 27)
Oak Run Studios
888 Marsh Cut-Off, Box 499
Mosier, OR 97040
(541) 478-3451

TINKA JORDY (PAGE 70)
Gardendance Studio
1902 Borland Road
Hillsborough, NC 27278
(919) 968-0884
tinka@garden-art.com

BOB KEEGAN (PAGE 12)
Classic Productions
927 Mt. Eyre
Newtown, PA 18940
(800) 543-8330
www.alpine-art.com

KEEYLA MEADOWS (PAGE 103)
Gardens & Art
1137 Stannage Avenue
Albany, CA 94706
(510) 524-7106

DAVID H.G. ROGERS (PAGE 56)
PO Box 486
Glenwood Landing, NY 11547
(516) 759-6422

CYR WILLIAM SMITH (PAGE 60)
Smith & York, Inc.
PO Box 175
Green Lake, WI 54941
(920) 294-0591

SANDY STRAGNELL (PAGE 49)
Sanford & Father Unlimited
5287 Bluff Head Road
Huletts Landing, NY 12841
(518) 499-0778

LYMAN WHITAKER (PAGE 117)
881 Coyote Gulch
Ivins, UT 84738
(435) 628-7467
windancer@sginet.com

THANKS

This book could not have happened without the help of some terrific people. First, special thanks to the contributing designers who created projects for the book (see page 126), as well as to the artists who allowed us to use photographs of their work in the gallery section (see page 127). Thanks also to those who kindly opened their gardens to our staff: Chris Bryant, Mark Burleson, Joel Cole, Dana Irwin, Katherine Kaderabek, Todd Kaderabek, Susan Kinney, Christopher Mello, Tommy Metcalf, Marla Murphy, Carol Parks, Bee Seiburg, Terry Taylor, Skip Wade, and Jeff Webb. The folks at Grovewood Gallery (Asheville, NC) and Garden Art Gallery (Chapel Hill, NC) were extremely helpful in providing useful information concerning a number of garden artists.

I would like to extend my appreciation to the following people at Lark Books who assisted me with putting the book together: Dana Irwin, for her expert advice and problem-solving skills; Antoine Peterson, for his endless carting and carrying; and Heather Smith, who was invaluable to the project from start to finish (especially in organizing the gallery section). I am exceedingly grateful to art director Chris Bryant and photographer Evan Bracken, who were joys to work with—even during more than a few days of unpredictable (and quite hot) location photography. Thanks also to Catharine Sutherland, Thom Gaines, and Cindy Burda. For his constant assistance and many kind gestures, special thanks to Patrick Doran.